MW01233857

An Accidental Lawyer

Also by Michael Melton

"Garage Band Days, a Memoir"

An Accidental Lawyer

Another Memoir

Michael Melton

ARCHWAY
PUBLISHING

Archway Publishing books may be ordered through booksellers or by contacting:

Archway Publishing
1663 Liberty Drive
Bloomington, IN 47403
www.archwaypublishing.com
844-669-3957

Because of the dynamic nature of the Internet, any web addresses or links contained in
this book may have changed since publication and may no longer be valid. The views
expressed in this work are solely those of the author and do not necessarily reflect the
views of the publisher, and the publisher hereby disclaims any responsibility for them.

Any people depicted in stock imagery provided by Getty Images are
models, and such images are being used for illustrative purposes only.
Certain stock imagery © Getty Images.

ISBN: 978-1-6657-6440-7 (sc)
ISBN: 978-1-6657-6441-4 (hc)
ISBN: 978-1-6657-6442-1 (e)

Library of Congress Control Number: 2024916906

Print information available on the last page.

Archway Publishing rev. date: 09/25/2024

This book is dedicated with much love to my incredible grandkids; Katie, William, Makenzi, and Mandi

I shall be telling this with a sigh
Somewhere ages and ages hence:
Two roads diverged into a wood, and I -
I took the one less traveled by,
And that has made all the difference.

-Robert Frost

CONTENTS

OPENING ARGUMENT

A favorite poet of mine, Bob Dylan, spoke about how your life can be changed by 'A Simple Twist of Fate.' I experienced several such twists in my life.

I had never been in a courtroom, had never seen a trial, did not know any lawyers, and had never watched Perry Mason.

All my prior occupations, several of which arrived unexpectedly, combined to lead me to becoming a trial lawyer, a job that had never been on my radar.

Until it was.

The first trial I ever saw I was in, representing a plaintiff in civil court. Lost that first one but got better at the craft and came to love the work of a trial lawyer.

This Memoir tells how my many twists of fate led to this fascinating career.

CHAPTER 1

The First Twenty-Two Years

I was born Charles Michael Melton on March 26, 1946. My brother, Ronald Evans Melton, came in on August 23, 1947. We were best friends from the beginning.

Our mom and dad, Lillian and Henry Melton, grew up in the small mining town of Whitwell, Tennessee. Dad was born in 1918, the fourth of six children. When he was six years old, his mom died in childbirth. His dad, Arden 'Pappy' Melton, had to quit his coal mining job because there was no one to care for the newborn baby. The family was evicted from their two-room shack because it belonged to the mining company, so they moved into a tent on the banks of the Sequachie River.

Whitwell is in Sequachie Valley, located across Signal Mountain from Chattanooga. My dad said the valley was so small, you could stand in the middle, reach out your arms, and touch the mountains on both sides. Growing up, our family made many pilgrimages to the valley to visit family and friends. His description was about right.

My mom's parents were Charles Evans Lockhart and Leona

Williams Lockhart. Mom was born in Eldorado, Illinois in 1923 where her dad worked in the mines as a carpenter. The mines there played out when she was one year old, and the family relocated to Whitwell. Rather than going back into the mines, Mr. Lockhart built a general store and gas station, with rooms in the back where the family lived.

Mom didn't know the Melton family, but she was aware they were suffering. She asked her mother if she could make a basket of food from the store and take it down to them. This was the first time my mom and dad met. He was nine years old, and my mom was just five.

Dad dropped out of school in the eighth grade to work and help provide for his family, eventually being hired by the Civilian Conservation Corps created by President Roosevelt during the Great Depression. Mom was singing for a living in a country band called 'Crabgrass,' appearing regularly on a local radio station. She passed down her love for music to her sons.

Eventually, they became a couple. Dad joined the Army at the start of World War II when he was twenty-two, and was shipped to Fort Ord, California for basic training. He was scheduled to shortly be transported to the battlefields of Africa and Europe. Mom could not let him leave without seeing him again, so she took a three-day bus ride from Tennessee to California. They located a preacher who married them, a week before dad shipped out.

She rode a bus back to Tennessee, and he rode a ship to Africa to serve in General Patton's army. His unit fought across North Africa, then Sicily, Italy, France, and Germany.

His company ended up in Hitler's mountaintop estate, the Eagle's Nest, outside of Berlin. Germany had been defeated.

Dad said his company spent three days in the mansion's wine cellar. After three years of combat, he said it was a nice break from the war.

Dad made it back home and I was born nine months later.

In looking for employment, dad was offered a job by a railroad company, and the Britling Cafeteria Company. The railroad's salary and benefits were much greater than that offered by Britling, but it required him to travel and be away from home for many days at a time. After being gone for over three years in the war, he found this unacceptable.

Dad went to work for the Britling Cafeteria Company, and mom went to birthing sons, four in all. There was me, Ronnie, Randy and Phillip. Music was always on in our home, particularly country music. But they also loved Elvis. The first album they ever bought was 'Blue Hawaii.'

Ronnie and I had taken piano lessons from ages five to twelve, as did Randy and Phillip. This classical music didn't really interest us. The piano teacher, Ms. Turner, held monthly piano recitals with her students, to show them off to the parents who were paying for the lessons. We were assigned solo pieces to memorize and play, and as siblings we were also required to play a duet. This was fun, we would subtly try to mess each other up without Ms. Turner catching on. We both learned to improvise during these duet duels.

Along with piano lessons, Nannie, our grandmother, bought us an accordion and a year's worth of lessons. At my size and weight, this was like wearing a piano on my chest, and I've never played one since.

Ronnie and I joined our local Boy Scout Troop 276. There were forty boys in our troop, and several of the boys' fathers were the scout masters. Our weekly meetings were held in the gym at Barrett Elementary School where we all attended. The troop went on a camping trip once a month, and one summer we camped out in tents for two weeks in the Smoky Mountains. One prank we liked to pull when we had a new recruit on his first camping trip was called a snipe hunt. The rookie would be set up in a tree with a paper sack and told to stay there until he captured a snipe in his bag.

There were no snipes in our area.

I reached the rank of First-Class Senior Patrol Leader and was asked to be a mentor to a Cub Scout Pack. One of the cubs was Mike Coppage who later in life became a Chief of Police while I was a city attorney. I loved telling him that I had given him his moral compass when we were both scouts.

Best troop ever.

My dad got two weeks paid vacation every summer. We alternated our destination every year between Panama City, Florida and Gatlinburg, Tennessee. Every trip was special, we were either swimming or hiking depending on which summer excursion we were on. We loved horseback riding in the Smokies and riding the waves at the beach. Gatlinburg was a strange city, numerous souvenir shops and no grocery store. Mom always made our meals in the motel room; restaurants were just too expensive for our budget.

I promise I saw this in one of the shops. There were Native Americans everywhere in town, and I was looking at a tomahawk. The tag on the one I was holding said, 'Made in Japan by Cherokee Indians.' I swear.

My mom and dad taught us about equality and diversity, through actions more than words. And this was in Alabama, in the 1950s. It appeared contradictory to what a kid would hear at that place and time. Dad told us about his father, Pappy, who had been a coal miner. The miners lived in a neighborhood of integrated coal company shacks. Dad said that the black and white miners would go underground for their shift, and when they came back up ten hours later, they were all black. There was no room for racial prejudice, they were all in the same circumstance.

When Ronnie and I were pre-school age, every Friday Miss Bessie was hired to come to our house to do my mom's ironing. We sat under the ironing board all day while Miss Bessie would talk and sing to us. My mom fixed sandwiches and we would all sit at the kitchen table for lunch. One Friday, my dad got home a little early and told Miss Bessie he would drive her home instead of her having to take the bus. I wanted to go too, so when we got to the car, I headed to the front door, and Miss Bessie to the back. Dad said, "Mikey, you get in the back seat, Miss Bessie is going to ride up front with me." Miss Bessie seemed a little reluctant, but dad insisted. It was many years later before I understood the dynamics of that event, the courage of my dad and Miss Bessie at that time and place.

Britling Cafeteria where my dad worked had a liberal system regarding race in hiring employees and was proposing a policy of serving any customer regardless of race. One morning we found a cross, about five feet tall, that had been burned in our front yard. My mom, brothers and I were very alarmed. My dad said. "Anyone who can do this without even waking you up is no one to be afraid of." We knew that Mr. Ruckus, who lived two doors down from us, was a Ku Klux Klan member. My dad had spent three years in combat in World War II, and although he was very reserved, he feared no man. He pulled the burnt cross out of the ground, and we saw him heading toward the Ruckus house. Dad came back shortly, without the cross. He never told us what had happened with Ruckus, but we never had another cross burned in our yard.

And they were Kennedy democrats, which was rare in this state.

In elementary school I played Pop Warner League football, like little league baseball, only with pads. I loved the sport and tried out for the Woodlawn High School football team my freshman year. Didn't happen. The coach asked me how much I weighed, and I proudly said "120 pounds." Then he said, "See that big guy over there? His nickname is 'Earthquake' and he will kill you. Take up tennis." I mourned for a few days, and then took up the sport with another freshman, Clint Frey. We spent many hours on an old asphalt tennis court teaching ourselves how to play. As juniors and seniors, both Clint and I played and lettered on the varsity tennis team.

Take that, coach.

We enjoyed the country music mom and dad loved, but we were much more interested in what we were hearing on our transistor radio. They called it rock and roll. We liked Elvis, Buddy Holly, Carl Perkins, and Jerry Lee Lewis. But our favorites were the Black artists; Chuck Berry, Little Richard, John Lee Hooker, Jimmy Reed, B.B. King, and Muddy Waters. They were the real deal.

The 1950s became the 1960s, and the curtain began to rise on a whole new world, powered by music. I would not trade being a teenager during that decade for any other time in history.

Around 1960, Ronnie and I decided we needed guitars. This instrument was obviously the prime mover of rock.

Dad never made much money, but he managed to support a family of six as the food buyer and warehouse manager for Britling, which at one time had nine locations. Mom was frugal, as most Great Depression veterans were. We never felt poor. They always found a way to get what we needed, and more important to us, what we really wanted. Ronnie and I each got a guitar for Christmas 1961. Mine was a Harmony archtop hollow body with a pickup, and Ronnie got a Silvertone solid body with a built-in amplifier in the case.

We began trying to figure out how they worked. There wasn't a guitar instructor available, so our source of instruction was a book of chords and the AM radio.

The 1960s was the perfect time for teens to form what were called garage bands. Instruments were inexpensive, and there were many venues for young groups to play.

Every Friday and Saturday evening, local bands would play at the skating rinks, National Guard Armories, theaters, and any location with a stage. Ronnie and I went to many of these shows and studied the local bands playing there; the Chambrays, the Premieres, the Rocking Rebellions, the Distortions, Rooster and the Townsmen, and the Torquays. My favorite local band was the Ramrods with Johnny Mulkey on lead guitar, and Freddie Guarino on drums. A few years later, his cousin, Jasper Guarino, would become our drummer, replacing Dailey when he was inducted into the Army.

I picked up chord progressions watching Johnny play, and I picked up envy watching the girls watching Johnny.

Theoretically, the garage was a great place to practice

without annoying the parents. We were even more fortunate. Our garage was about fifty feet from the house and had a two-room apartment attached to it. My parents called it the 'rumpus room.' I have no idea where that name came from, but it was the perfect place for a new band to get organized.

We talked a couple of friends, Ray and Danny Lofton, who had no musical background, into joining us. We began working on being a band good enough to play the rink on a Friday night. Ray got a set of drums, Danny a bass guitar and amp. Then we found thirteen-year-old Ron Parr, already a great guitarist. We met him when he was performing a solo act at a local senior center, wearing a too big sports coat and playing a too big acoustic guitar, covering Buddy Holly songs. We told him about our plans, and he agreed to join. Ron had a neighbor, Eddie Eubanks, who could sing the blues. I became the rhythm guitarist and Ronnie was on keyboard. We named our band The Tempos.

One show was all we wanted. The band worked hard together, practicing in the rumpus room every chance we could. One other interesting feature, there was a switch in the house by the back door that controlled the power to the rumpus room. I remember us starting on a new song, and when Eddie sang the line 'shake your money maker,' the power suddenly went out. My mom was listening closer than we thought, so that song didn't make the cut. By March of 1963, we felt we were ready to audition. We had a setlist of sixteen songs. I talked with a member of one of the local bands, and he gave me a suggestion about how to get booked.

He said, "Make a business card for the band and take it to the skating rink manager. He'll figure that if you have a business card, you must be good enough to play the rink." It worked! He booked the band for a show in June 1963.

Matching outfits were mandatory for bands, so we decided on black sports coats and gray slacks. We met at Ron's house before the show. Seeing the band under the streetlight wearing the same outfit and heading out for our first gig was incredible. That Friday night went by in a blur of excitement. The Tempos had accomplished its goal. We had played the rink.

We didn't stop there. The Tempos kept practicing, got better, and stayed busy. We were now a popular blues band. In addition to the rinks, we were hired to play a few bars. The most unusual was the Allstate Club north of Birmingham.

After arriving and loading in, we noticed that there was a wall of chicken wire on the front of the stage. Obviously, some incident in the past required a wall to protect the band from flying objects. We played anyway, and although the band was never a target, we heard that someone in the bar lost an ear that night. You were not in good hands at this Allstate. We never went back.

FEBRUARY 9, 1964.

If you were a teenager in the 1960s, you know exactly what happened that night.

The Beatles played five songs on the Ed Sullivan Show. Everything about music changed, and so did we. Ron, Ronnie and I wanted to take up this new music. It just wouldn't work with our lineup, so the three of us left the Tempos.

We started looking for musicians who were interested in this style of music. We found Dailey Vandegriff, a good drummer, who left his band to join us. Then, singer and songwriter Michael Gunnels joined, bringing rhythm guitarist Mike Pair with him from their band, The Illusions. I switched to bass guitar, and we were ready to rock. Now we needed a new name for our band. I was a fan of Charles Dickens and suggested the titles of two of his books for consideration, *Great Expectations*, and *Hard Times*. Hard Times won the vote. A couple of years later, our record company advised we had to change our name because there was another band in California that had prior rights to it. What are the odds.

I recalled a piece I had played during a piano recital. The composer was Igor Stravinsky, and the work was 'The Rites of Spring.' And that became our new name.

Before long, we were playing locally, then state-wide, and then around the country. Within five years, we had become a very popular band. We signed a recording contract with Cameo-Parkway Records, with its studios in Philadelphia. We signed a booking and management contract with the Bill Lowery Talent Agency in Atlanta. And then, for a band that had been satisfied just getting to play a one-off at a skating rink, we flew to Los Angeles and filmed an episode of Dick Clark's national TV show 'Where the Action Is.'

By 1967 we had played hundreds of shows and had been honored to play on stage with some of the most famous groups of the day, like Herman's Hermits, and the Animals.

On one occasion, we opened for The James Gang. A girl named Carolyn Fitzgerald attended with her best friend Patty Crick. I believe Patty was seeing someone with the band and had brought Carolyn to introduce her to someone else with the group.

But I saw her first. And a couple of years later we were married.

One concert stands out more than any other. We opened a show starring the godfather of rock and roll, Jerry Lee Lewis. He was one of our heroes. After we played and it was time for Jerry Lee, he staggered out of his dressing room, obviously under the influence. But when he got on stage, his set was perfect. He rocked the house.

On another occasion, we were asked to be the backup band for blues artist Arthur Alexander, so we learned all his songs. Our roadies loaded in at the concert venue in Birmingham, and we were ready to go. Then we were told Arthur had been arrested on his way to the show, apparently on a DUI charge, and would not be joining us.

Dan Brennan from radio station WVOK had located a replacement, Tommy Roe, who was also playing in Birmingham and said he could come over and do a set of his hits.

We had thirty minutes to learn his songs. Ron Parr figured out the chord progression in his head for Tommy's biggest hit, 'Sheila,' and passed it on to the rest of us. Then we asked about his other songs. Ron smiled, and said, "They're all the same." And so, we served as the backup band for Tommy Roe, an artist who once had The Beatles open for him in England.

A year later, we were in Los Angeles preparing to film our segment for the 'Where the Action Is' show. We were all sitting in make-up chairs getting properly groomed, when Tommy Roe came in and took the chair next to mine. He was also getting ready to film a segment that day. We had a great conversation, and he remembered the night when we backed him up, telling me we did a great job on his songs.

There was now no limit to how far we could continue to move up in the music industry. The government saw it differently. It had decided to have a war in Viet Nam, and by the end of 1967 most of us had been drafted. We had one more show together, a goodbye to our fans, in December 1967, and the journey was over.

Ron Parr, our talented lead guitar player and songwriter, was trained to drive a tank, and then sent to war. Six weeks after he arrived in Viet Nam, his tank rolled over a landmine, and he was killed. Ron was thirteen when the band started. He was nineteen when he died. But in those five years, traveling the country and making music, Ron, and the rest of us, had lived a lifetime.

CHAPTER 2

The United States Air Force

Going to school while playing in a traveling band finally proved impossible. I was enrolled at Samford University near Birmingham and finished three and a half years there by missing the maximum number of classes allowed while maintaining a low 'C' average. In December 1966, I was flying back and forth between shows and final exams, and that was just too much to handle. I didn't enroll for the 1967 spring semester because our band's agent, Cotton Carrier (cool name) with the Bill Lowery Talent Agency, had booked us solid for the year.

The only reason I was trying to maintain school enrollment was to keep my student deferment from the draft. I knew that I was likely to be drafted, but I made a difficult decision to do it anyway.

The year 1967 was now totally dedicated to making music, and it was wonderful. On the road full time. Dailey was the first to enter the service, in the summer of 1967. We found Jasper Guarino, another great drummer, to be his replacement. Then, that winter, Ron Parr was drafted, and we knew this was the end of our dream for success in this crazy business of rock and roll. As I previously noted, The Rites of Spring had a final concert in December in Birmingham for our many fans. This was the end, but a wonderful way to go out.

Having passed my physical for the draft in July, I knew my number would be called up. I did not want to be drafted into the Army and be sent to fight in a useless war. I went to talk to the Air Force recruiter to see what he had to offer. As it turned out, they were looking for people to be assigned to the Air Force Intelligence Service in Washington, D.C. That sounded interesting, particularly the part about never having to leave the country during what would be a four-year enlistment. I left the recruiter to think about his proposal.

Exactly one week later, I was back in his office showing him what I had just received in the mail. It was an Order to report for induction on January 9,1969 into the Army of the United States of America. It was a very scary piece of paper. But the recruiter came through. He said that if I was sworn in to the Air Force before January 9, the draft notice would become void. I was sworn into active duty in the United States Air Force on January 2, 1969. I soon shipped out by bus to Lackland Air Force Base near San Antonio, Texas for two months of Basic Training.

My brother Ronnie received his draft notice around the same time I did. Our dad offered us an out from the war. He said, "I didn't spend three years of my life in combat so that my sons would have to fight in a stupid war." He said that he would pay our way to Canada if we wanted out.

We both opted to take non-combat service and avoid the penalties involved in draft dodging. Ronnie, in the most unusual set of circumstances I ever saw in the military system, became a piano player. In the Army. Somehow, he found out there was something called the Allied Forces European Symphony Orchestra, and they were taking auditions for a pianist. Ronnie applied, got the gig, and spent two years traveling around Europe playing classical music. Our many years of music lessons kept him out of a war. He told me the most fun in this job was getting to drive the bus, because they had no speed limits in Europe.

Back to me. I got to Lackland AFB, had my head shaved, was issued some unstylish uniforms, and settled into the barracks. The days consisted of long marches, obstacle courses, classroom training, and considerable yelling by our Training Instructor.

I was also taught to take apart and reassemble an M-16 rifle. In my pre-military life, I had never fired a gun of any kind. My dad had frequently taken all his sons fishing, but never hunting. He said this wasn't a sport for him because as a child he had to hunt to get food for his family.

With no prior experience involving firearms, on the range I shot expert in the four firing positions: prone, sitting, kneeling, and standing. The Air Force gave me a nice ribbon to hang on my uniform. I don't know where I got that skill, and I haven't fired a gun since.

After completion of basic training, I was shipped to Keesler AFB in Mississippi to receive the classroom training I would need in my job in the Intelligence Service. Carolyn joined me there and we rented a small one-story apartment, in a connected group of four. No one was renting the apartment directly next to us, which turned out to be fortuitous. In trying to defrost the refrigerator's little freezer, I accidentally punctured the tube housing the freon. Now we had no freezer, and I expected the apartment manager would make me pay for the damage. We came up with a solution. Somehow, Carolyn and I moved our wounded refrigerator to the empty apartment next door and relocated the one there to our place. Problem solved.

Keesler AFB was also a training facility for South Vietnamese Air Force pilots. I became accustomed to the constant drone of the WWII prop engine aircraft being used for this training. They often landed off the runway, and sometimes in the Gulf. It made me glad I wasn't in pilot training there.

At my graduation on September 8, 1969, I received a Certificate from Air Training Command naming me an Honor Graduate. That was nice, considering my 'C' average career at Samford. I also got a letter of congratulations from Lt. Col. Lynn E. Atwood, welcoming me to the 1127th Field Activity Group. This was getting serious.

The unit was located at Fort Belvoir, Virginia, just south of Washington. Carolyn and I packed up and headed toward my assignment. Everything we owned was in the car, a black and white TV, a stereo, and our clothes. We knew that there was no on-base housing available, so we had to figure out how to live on the economy in the second highest cost of living area in the country.

I had a couple of days before I was due to report. My cousin David Anderson was also in the Air Force and stationed at the Pentagon. He and his wife were living in an apartment complex near D.C. and there was an unfurnished one-bedroom apartment available in the same complex. It was September and Carolyn was pregnant with our first child, due in December. We signed a lease for the apartment, the rent was $120 a month. Our car payment at the time was $72 and my monthly pay rate as an Airman First Class was a grand total of $380 before taxes. Do the math.

We moved in, put our clothes in a pile, covered it with a sheet, and that's where we slept for several weeks.

I quickly learned that military personnel, such as me, took part time jobs to supplement their modest military income. With the help of fellow airmen, I found a part-time job with the Sears Landmark store, and with the additional income we bought three rooms of furniture for $299. Not great but serviceable.

On the designated date in my Orders, I reported to my new post. It consisted of a large compound, surrounded by a tall chain-link fence topped with razor wire.

Armed sentries patrolled outside the fence all the time, day and night. Inside the compound was a line of ten former barracks buildings that had been converted into offices. I met the officers and enlisted airmen assigned to my building and was shown the desk where I would be working for the next three years.

During that time, I made close friends, particularly with the young personnel that had been selected for this assignment like I had been. It didn't take long to understand the incredible mission with which this group was tasked. In the 1127th Field Activity Group, the Field was the world, and the Activity was gathering covert intelligence. Everything we did was coordinated with other intelligence services, particularly the ones located at the Pentagon.

The compound also had some unusual amenities. There were numerous trees where squirrel families lived. They were not afraid of people. On one occasion, when the door was open, a mama squirrel came in, carrying her baby in her mouth, and climbed up on my desk. She put it down, and looked up at me as if saying, "Isn't my baby cute?"

Next to our building was a picnic table and a horseshoe pit.

Lunch was fun there, talking and pitching a few games. There was also a storage room full of camping equipment for us to use at no charge. Carolyn and I borrowed a tent, lamp, Coleman stove, and tent heater, and went camping in the Appalachian Mountains. It was winter and snow flurries made the trip beautiful. Kevin was about three months old and seemed to enjoy the trip.

I know most people are aware of the levels of military classification: Confidential, Secret, and Top Secret. I don't think many know about two more classifications above Top Secret: Top Secret No Forn and Top Secret Crypto. Everyone in the 1127th had to be cleared for this highest classification. The crypto designation refers to cryptology, or codes. The codes for transmitting data worldwide are the most guarded of all information in the intelligence community. I later heard from everyone I had ever known that they had been visited by the FBI, checking me out. I apparently passed the audition.

In the middle of the compound was a burn pit. At the end of each workday, all paperwork that wasn't to be locked in a safe overnight was stuffed into a red and white striped burn bag. Even typewriter ribbons were burned every day.

My job description said that I would 'perform all actions relative to the reassignment of officer personnel of this unit, DIA, DSA and the Air Force Attache system. Involves notifications to selected personnel, scheduling training involved and compliance with any peculiar assignment instructions. Makes travel requests, monitors sponsorship for outgoing, and performs as the OPR for the Overseas Project Officer.'

You can read between the lines. Theoretically, I could be involved in a project, maybe sending assets by submarine, then rubber raft to a foreign country 'to check things out.' Not saying that happened.

One mission I remember well. I'm still not allowed to talk about it because of the methods and assets classification. Three things resulted from this mission; I was promoted to Sergeant, I was awarded the Air Force Commendation Medal, and I received an invitation to the White House.

I got the notice of this invitation from Colonel Maynard L. Mayberry, Executive Secretary of the Air Force to attend a reception hosted by President Nixon in the Rose Garden for His Excellency Hilman Baumsgaard, the Prime Minister of Denmark. I also got to tour the White House, even checking out the Oval Office. Just walked in, looked around, and walked out, thanks to my crypto clearance.

Our son Kevin was born at the Fort Belvoir hospital on December 10, 1969. Carolyn and I bought two bicycles and put a child carrier on the back of her bike. Every Sunday, we packed a lunch and rode out. The bike paths from our apartment in Alexandria ran north into Washington along the Potomac River. This route was beautiful, and in the spring was lined with cherry blossoms in bloom. Arriving in Washington, we would lock our bikes and tour the monuments and museums. At Christmas, the town was decorated with the national Christmas tree, and a tree representing every state.

We often had family visit us and would take them on a guided tour. As many trips as we made to Washington, we still never saw it all.

Other times, we headed south on the Mount Vernon Parkway, where on Sundays, two lanes of the road were closed to cars for bike riders to use. Biking was a popular activity in Washington, hundreds of people would be on this road every Sunday. Touring George Washington's home at Mount Vernon seven miles down the road was always a great ride.

Those Sundays were the best days of my tour.

Both of my jobs were interesting. I became the night supervisor in the Sears credit department with sixteen men and women in the service working there part-time like me. In those days, a Sears Credit account had to be in the city where the cardholder lived. The population of the D.C. area was in constant flux, with military and political personnel moving in and out daily. The department was constantly busy, particularly at night and Saturday, with people transferring their accounts. There were sixteen windows where an employee and the customer would fill out an application for transfer and then bring it back to me. I would call the Sears store where the account was located and get a report on its status and credit limit. If everything checked out, I could approve the transfer, set a limit, and issue a temporary card.

On one occasion, someone brought back a completed application with the name 'Wernher Von Braun' on it. I couldn't believe it. I asked the clerk to bring him back to the office so I could meet him. He said that he had just been transferred to ·Washington from Huntsville, Alabama. Mr. Braun worked as the NASA Engineering Program Manager and was the chief architect of the Apollo Saturn V rocket. I didn't bother calling the Huntsville Sears. After chatting for a couple of minutes, I gave him a temporary card with the maximum limit I was allowed to make.

On the military side, something happened that I could never have imagined. As it was told to me, the DIA was making a film about the ways intelligence agencies conducted investigations under various circumstances. I'm not even sure who the film was being made for, possibly legislators on the appropriate committees. For some reason, I have no idea why, I was asked to be in one of the segments. It sounded like fun, so I said yes and took the part.

Here's the deal on my role. I'm a Russian bomber pilot who strayed too close to the U.S. east coast. My plane is shot down, I parachute out and land in the woods, where I am captured. The people producing the film sent a coach to prepare me for the role and give me a Russian pilot's uniform to wear for my scene. I also got some tips on using a Russian accent.

I was to meet the film crew and director on a certain morning at Andrews AFB and be carried in a Huey helicopter to an army fort near the wooded area where my scene would be filmed. I showed up at Andrews that morning, got passed in by the guard at the entrance, and parked. I got out of the car, put the uniform under my arm, and began walking to the designated building. I suddenly realized there might be a problem. I'm walking no further than one hundred feet from Air Force One, carrying a Russian Officer's uniform. Nobody said a word, great security there I guess.

We loaded onto the Huey and headed south. On the flight, I learned something new. Helicopters are very, very loud and we had to wear ear mufflers. This information would turn out to be useful many years later.

On the flight, I changed into my Russian Pilot's uniform, and somebody put makeup on me to simulate minor injuries. After landing, we hiked to the location in the woods where my segment would be filmed.

Action! And the show began. I was dragged out of the woods by a couple of soldiers and propped against a stump. An interrogator knelt and began questioning me, and I responded with my memorized script and best Russian accent.

This took about an hour and then we were transported to the Army mess hall for lunch. I had the opportunity to ask the Director what he thought of my Russian accent. "Fine," he said, "if you were from southern Russia." I had been advised that he was a famous Hollywood Director, 'Wolfgang' something. He didn't ask me to star in any of his movies though.

I never got to see the film, which I understood had eight segments. The only thing that trumps Crypto is 'need to know.' This rule applies to all classified data in the military, no matter your level of clearance, you must also have a specific need to know the classified information.

On October 19, 1971, Commander, Department of the Air Force, Colonel Milton Bellovin named me the Airman of the Quarter. I can't remember why, but I still have the Certificate.

There was a great benefit provided to members of the military called The Commissary. This was a grocery store for service members and had incredibly low prices. I remember one occasion when we went to a big commissary in D.C. This store had about sixty checkout lanes. Carolyn and I each filled a grocery cart to overflowing, enough food for a month. The tab was $68.

It turned out to be a great experience, this military job. There is great camaraderie between service members, we're all on the same mission.

I was mustered out of the Air Force on December 7, 1972. Carolyn, Kevin, and I moved back to Birmingham.

CHAPTER 3

A Pseudo Mechanic

And now, I'm a veteran. An unemployed veteran. My primary goal was to finish my studies at Samford University and earn a bachelor's degree. I enrolled for the 1973 spring semester and scheduled all morning classes. This meant changing my major from English to Sociology, but hey, what's the difference? I was hoping a diploma in anything would lead to what I referred to in my mind, as a 'tie' job. No particular occupation, I just knew that if I had a job that required wearing a tie, it would be indoors and involve no heavy lifting.

Unable to find employment despite several leads, I talked to my uncle, Bobby Carroll. He was the regional manager for the Firestone Tire Company. Uncle Bobby offered to hire me as a mechanic at the Firestone store in downtown Birmingham.

I am not, nor have I ever been a mechanic.

I said yes and took the job. The schedule worked out well, I attended Samford classes in the morning and my Firestone job in the afternoon.

The main business of Firestone is the sale of tires. This part of the job was easy to learn. Pry the old tire off the rim and the new one on, then balance and mount it on the car.

However, we also did tune-ups, alignments, and brake replacements. My first brake job seemed to work out alright, except that I had about five parts left over. The brakes seemed to work okay though.

On another occasion, I was charged with replacing a water pump. I think it was on a Buick. No problem. The pump was easy to get to, and I only had to remove four bolts and the hoses. So far, so good. I set the new pump in place and started putting in the long, skinny bolts. As I screwed the first bolt in, waiting for it to get tight, the head snapped off. I had the same result with the other bolts. After hooking up the hoses, I turned the engine on, and the new pump worked correctly. Then another mechanic, a real one, introduced me to the torque wrench, a tool that could be adjusted to tighten the bolts without having to pop the heads off. He also told me, "That's probably the last water pump this car will ever have."

One other incident of note. The store had a policy for a brake inspection. We would check the brakes and advise the customer of their condition. If the customer didn't want a brake job at that time, they would be charged one dollar for the inspection.

On this occasion, I inspected a car's brakes and advised the customer that they were shot, worn out. He wasn't prepared to pay for new brakes and went into the showroom to pay his dollar. I thought it would be a good idea to back his car out of the garage and pull it up in front of the store for the customer's convenience. Backing out, the brakes seemed to be working. However, when I started moving forward toward the showroom, no brakes at all. I was furiously pumping the brake pedal as the car moved toward the store, jumping the curb, and crashing through the big plate-glass floor to ceiling window. I was now sitting in a car in the middle of the showroom.

The customer and manager stared at me in disbelief, as they completed the dollar inspection fee transaction. No words were spoken. I got out, the customer got in, backed out, and left. The manager and I discussed the situation. Apparently, he was a little miffed. He made me spend the night in the store because the window replacement could not be installed until the next day.

I told you I wasn't a mechanic.

One day I was putting four tires on a car when the customer began talking to me about my future. I had finished my last semester at Samford and received my diploma, the first college degree in my family. Also, I had been receiving tuition benefits through the GI Bill, three hundred and eighty-five tax free dollars a month. I was entitled to four years of this benefit, and had only used half a year, but I had no thoughts of pursuing higher education.

He introduced himself, Jack McCarn, a vice president with a major real estate and insurance company, Johnson, Rast and Hays. I discussed my history with him. Jack said "You know, I went to a law school that holds its evening classes in the courtrooms of the Jefferson County Courthouse. It's called The Birmingham School of Law." Jack knew the Dean, Hugh Locke, Jr., whose father had founded the school in 1915.

He said if I wanted to go there and keep receiving the veteran's benefits, he would put in a good word for me with the Dean. In my mind, having a law degree meant very little, I never planned to be a lawyer, but receiving those monthly checks meant a lot.

And then Jack McCarn offered me a job with Johnson, Rast

and Hays. The position would be in the insurance section, and I would be the agent handling their new product, surety and fidelity bonds. I had never heard of these things before.

I said, 'Yes, when do I start." This random meeting, as would other such events in the future, changed the course of my life.

CHAPTER 4

Surety and Fidelity Bond Agent (a tie job)

I started work with Johnson, Rast and Hays a couple of days later. Jack helped me get admitted to the Birmingham School of Law, beginning classes in September 1973. I completed the Veterans Administration paperwork necessary to continue my GI Bill benefits. One month's check paid for a semester's tuition and books; the rest was profit.

Now I'm a law school student.

JR&H was not handling surety and fidelity bonds at that time. To get into selling these products, they purchased an existing company, Nelson & Crabbe, that specialized in bonds. I was assigned to temporarily work in that office situated a block from the courthouse. The owner, Bill Nelson, was to train me in the nuances of the products for a couple of months before he retired, and then his files would be transferred to the JR&H offices on Magnolia Avenue in the south side of Birmingham.

Nelson & Crabbe, being so close to the courthouse, had a

constant stream of lawyers purchasing surety bonds required in their guardianship cases in Probate Court.

Mr. Nelson was a very crabby, cantankerous man. He was angry that he was having to retire and sell the business he had built and operated for decades. He grudgingly educated me on bonds, how they were created, and what they covered. And he was constantly telling me about the 1928 Alabama football team when he was a student there. His hero was the quarterback, who he always referred to as 'the great Grant Gillis.' I heard that name a hundred times.

He had not been very good at hiring secretaries. The one working there when I started had been keeping company money in her desk, funds that had been paid by attorneys purchasing surety bonds with cash. She shortly disappeared, as did the cash, which Mr. Nelson estimated to be several thousand dollars.

Her replacement also had issues. It appeared she would have a few tequila sunrises before coming to work. She stayed pretty much hammered all day.

Back to business. These were not bail bonds. Surety bonds are posted by guardians and conservators who would be responsible for moneys and assets belonging to someone else, usually a minor, or incapacitated person. If they misappropriated the funds, the bond protected the estate. Fidelity bonds are purchased by builders, guaranteeing to the entity they contract with that if they fail to complete a project, the bond covers the cost to have it completed by another party.

Not as complicated as it sounds. Probably.

A couple of months later, Bill Nelson retired. The files, and me, were transferred to the home office on Magnolia Avenue. I was given a corner office close to Jack McCarn and next door to

Bob Hays, the partner in charge of the insurance division. I was the only agent handling these bonds.

It was arranged for me to be what is called an 'Attorney-in-Fact' for several insurance companies that would be making the actual product. One of these was the Travelers Insurance Company, where my sister-in-law Sally Bookout Melton was employed as an agent. We worked together on many projects, mostly fidelity bonds.

JR&H sent me to the University of Georgia in Athens to attend seminars on my new specialty. The lectures provided more detailed information than I had received from Bill Nelson, and better prepared me for the intricacies of writing bonds.

I learned a lot in this job, although it became tedious, doing the same thing day after day. At least I didn't have to do any brake jobs.

At lunch, several of us would eat in the park across the street and toss around a football.

Five nights a week I was in class. The first evening, I ran into another new law student, Ted Gideon, who had been my next-door neighbor growing up. We hadn't interacted much as kids; I was on the road a lot, playing in a traveling band when we were teenagers. More about Ted later.

Every evening, a specific area of the law was covered by the professors, from contracts to constitutional law, civil and criminal procedure, etc. A different lawyer taught each course, and they were well versed in their topic. Holding classes in a courtroom, with the professor sitting in the judge's chair, was the perfect location to study the law.

As a student, I was enjoying my G.I. Bill benefits, but still with no thought about becoming a lawyer.

CHAPTER 5

Time For Another Profession

I had been with Johnson, Rast and Hayes for a couple of years when I ran into Pat Garrett, a friend from high school. We talked about what we had been doing since graduating from Woodlawn. During our conversation, she told me about her employment with the Alabama Department of Human Resources as a Social Worker. Pat also mentioned that there was an opening at the Agency.

So, naturally, I applied for the opening. I scheduled an appointment and was interviewed by the Director, Doris Adwell. After reading my resume, she asked me about my varied work history. I mentioned that my former classmate had been the one who suggested that I apply. "Do you always say yes?" she asked.

"Yes," I replied.

I was hired. I left JR&H, and began my career as a Social Worker, once again getting up to speed on a totally new profession.

I was assigned a caseload of one hundred and thirty young, single women with children. The government, under the Aid to Dependent Children Act, provided a grand total of $150 per month to these young mothers, plus a small amount of food stamps.

Three days a week I would be in the field visiting my clients. The DHR required that I make a visit to each of my clients in their home at least once every six months. The other two days I spent in the office, writing reports on my home visits.

Most of my clients lived in a housing project in north Birmingham called Collegeville, an immense collection of two-story Section 8 apartments. They were living in poverty, as their families had for generations. They never experienced any other life, most believing that there was no way out of this cycle of poverty. That was my job, showing them the doors leading to a better life for their family.

I had many tools to offer, beginning with education. The focus was helping them earn a General Education Degree (GED) if they hadn't graduated from high school. The next step was vocational training, primarily in junior college. This was all new information to them, and I never had a client that didn't welcome the proposals I made to help overcome their life of poverty and hopelessness.

One of the first clients I visited was Ms. Snow, a mother of two children. Working with various agencies, she obtained a GED, and was admitted to Jefferson State Junior College. I located a daycare for her two pre-school sons. Every day, she would take the long trip to school, changing buses each way. By the end of my time with DHR, she had earned a Nurse's Assistant degree, found employment at Carraway Hospital, and moved her family out of the projects. Ms. Snow told me she had never thought any of this was possible.

This story of success happened many times. That was the reason I was here, to show clients what was possible. It felt good.

Another problem I discovered, the amount of food stamps a client received was nominal, and a client could run out of food before the end of the month. I would get a desperate call, usually on a Friday, asking me if there was food available until the first of the next month. I had a list of resources that provided food for the needy, helping them get through for a few days. The best resource, by far, was the Catholic Center of Concern. I could go by there, pick up a bag of mostly canned goods, and deliver it to my client. The Center received most of its stock from local grocery stores, primarily dented cans that had been removed from their shelves.

When the Center was low on stock, I had a list of other charities that contributed food to poverty-stricken families. I would go to one of the sites, get a bag of food and deliver it.

I learned that children in my own hometown were suffering from hunger. I had thought this only happened in other countries. I was wrong. But there were at least resources available if you knew how to access them. I learned to do that.

Another aspect of this job dealt with the Child Protective Services section of DHR. If I suspected that a child in my client group or outside of it was being abused, I would investigate, including interviewing witnesses. There was a separate unit specifically charged with this program, so I only handled a couple of these investigations.

I would complete a report about what I had learned concerning the possibility of abuse. I would submit the report to my supervisor for review, and then file it with the Jefferson County Family Court Judge. The Judge would then issue an Order authorizing me to remove the child from their home if the facts warranted. Following Protective Service's advice in these situations, I would ask two police officers to accompany me when I executed the Court's Order. I then took the child to the Foster Care Service agency pending further investigation by the District Attorney's office. A hearing would be set in Family Court, where I and other witnesses would testify. Based on the evidence presented, the Judge would make the appropriate decision about what was in the child's best interest.

I discovered another task of a Social Worker that no one had informed me about. On April 5, 1977, I received a phone call at 3:00am. A tornado had just hit Smithfield, a Birmingham neighborhood. The caller said that as a Social Worker, I was also an Emergency Services Worker. Well, that was a surprise. He instructed me to immediately proceed to Smithfield. Which I did.

There wasn't much I could contribute at this scene of incredible destruction other than help escort residents out of their destroyed and flooded homes, some by boat.

That was a specialty I hadn't anticipated in this job.

Meanwhile, I was still attending law school. My friend Ted Gideon and I had an evening routine. The classes ran from 6:00pm to 8:00pm. At the time, there was a restaurant across the street from the courthouse called Dale's. The restaurant is long gone, but you can still get Dale's Steak Sauce at your local grocery store. Ted and I would meet there before class started, order a glass of tea, and then fill up on the free appetizers. No one ever stopped us from eating as much as we wanted. Delicious.

One day Ted asked what I thought about being a wedding photographer on the weekends. As was my habit, I said "Yes." He bought a Yashica Matte, a camera that provided a 4"x4" negative allowing the printing of high-quality large prints. He named the business Amber Portraits after one of his daughters and had business cards printed. As the 'executive' he would handle the paperwork, get the photos printed, and sell them to the customer. That meant I was the wedding photographer. I shot about fifty weddings over the next year. They were always beautiful events, lots of happy people. Usually.

Kevin was nine years old and loved going to the weddings with me. I made him my 'tripod' man. He held onto the tripod until time for the 'set shots,' family pictures made after the ceremony. I knew the real reason Kevin loved these trips was the reception that would follow the wedding. He was often the first person in line at the food tables.

Kevin and I shot a wedding in a small town in northwest Alabama on a Christmas Eve. We were in my Pinto trying to get home and had become lost on a rural two-lane road. Pre-GPS. There was nothing around, no farms, no houses and no service stations. We were listening to the radio giving the latest reports on Santa's location. Kevin was very concerned that Santa would beat us home.

My plan now was to find a house with its lights on, knock on the door and ask for help and directions. We were very low on fuel. And then, a Christmas miracle! Around midnight, we ran into I-65, our route home, and an open service station. We beat Santa home.

Law school had become very interesting. I was learning about the evolution of our fantastic legal system. Still no thought about being a lawyer, just enjoying the classes, and, of course, a $385 check every month. The professors were all practicing attorneys in their day jobs, so we had the benefit of their class lessons, and their trial experiences.

CHAPTER 6

Law School's Over, Now What?

Suddenly, it's 1977 and I'm a Senior. That four years sure went by fast.

During my time as a law school student, Carolyn and I had welcomed a new member to the family. Ashley Elizabeth Melton was born in Birmingham on May 18, 1975.

My class elected me vice-president of the senior class. I didn't even know I was running. With this honor, I found that it carried the task of planning the graduation program and lining up a guest speaker. That involved quite a bit of work, but I got it handled. I graduated in May, 1977, and was continuing my employment as a Social Worker, a job intense but rewarding.

Sometime before the end of that last year, Ted talked with me about his plan to take the Bar Exam in February,1978. At that time, the Alabama Bar Exam was given twice a year, in February and July. The first one after our graduation was scheduled for July 1977. The word was that the bar exam in February was the best one to take because there were fewer candidates taking the test, for whatever that means.

Ted asked me if I wanted to ride down there with him, and maybe take the test myself.

I said yes, not sure why though.

But, if I was going to take the bar exam, I wanted to be ready for it. Ted was using his class notes and textbooks to study. I discovered there were other resources to help me prepare, companies that specialized in teaching students how to pass the bar exam. I selected one located in Chicago called the Nord Review. Everything was handled through the U.S. mail.

The Bar Exam lasts three days. The first two days consist of a series of fact situations for which you must set out the legal parameters of the case, and the applicable law, in essay form. Testing lasts eight hours each day, and these essay problems are long and complicated. The third day consists of one hundred multiple choice questions, referred to as the 'multi-state.' The questions are difficult, because all four choices are correct. The object is to select the answer which is the MOST correct. Not easy.

Nord sent me a package of sample essay questions that had been used on previous bar exams. I would complete a response, mail it back. Nord would grade it and let me know what I hit and what I missed. Of course, these samples would not actually be on the test. Only the Bar Examiners knew what the test questions would be, and they created new ones for each exam. These were just samples of past tests. Nord then sent me several multi-state exams that had been used before. I completed them and Nord would critique my answers, telling me why I was right on some and wrong on others. The more of these I took, the better my results.

I began to understand what the bar examiners were looking

for in essays and multi-state questions. The Nord experience gave me confidence, I felt ready for the test.

Bring it on.

Ted and I drove to Montgomery the day before the test and checked into a motel next to the venue where we would be tested. As Nord had recommended, I didn't do any studying that night. I knew they were right. If I wasn't ready by now, one more sweaty night of study would not make a difference. Instead, I sat back and relaxed. Ted and everybody else I saw were cramming.

The next morning, those of us taking the exam assembled, and the monitors gave us instructions on how the tests would be structured. The first essay question was handed out, a page and a half single-spaced. We were given one hour for each essay. All at once, I realized that even though I had never seen this set of facts before, I knew exactly how to answer it. Thank you, Nord!

On the second day, it was obvious that there were fewer test takers than the day before. On the final day, the multi-state, even more people had bailed.

And then it was over. Three days, eight hours each day, was mentally exhausting. Ted and I loaded into his car and headed north. We talked about the test, and while I was very upbeat about how I had done, Ted apparently wasn't quite as confident. "If you don't stop talking about how good you did, I'm going to pull over and put you out of the car!"

I kept quiet for the rest of the trip home.

Besides, I really had no reason to worry about whether I passed or not.

After all, I had no plans to be a lawyer.

CHAPTER 7

The Accident

The results of the Bar Exam were mailed out three months later in May 1978. I was told that if the envelope was thin, it would probably indicate I passed the test, but it wouldn't tell me what my score was. A thick one meant failure, and would contain the test grade, as well as the reasons for a failing score.

On May 18, 1978, Ashley's third birthday, I received a thin envelope. I had passed the Bar Exam. I would have a nice document to hang on the wall while I continued my job as a Social Worker.

And then, less than an hour after getting the letter, I received a call from one of my law school professors, Leo Costello, who had taught the class on Contracts. He had a successful plaintiffs' personal injury law firm in the Avondale neighborhood of Birmingham. Leo asked me if I had passed. I assumed he was just checking in with his former students.

I was wrong. I sensed an accident coming.

Leo said that he had just talked to Ted, who had also passed the Bar, and hired him to join his law firm. Ted accepted the job and suggested to Leo that I would be an asset to the firm. Would I be interested in the job?

Guess.

Time's up. I said "yes."

This was a Saturday morning. I told Leo that I would need to give DHR, my current employer, at least two weeks' notice that I was leaving my social worker job. Leo said, "No, I need you to start Monday." Two days away. Leo and Barbara Stott, his lady and the office manager, were leaving that day for a two-week vacation in Europe. He needed Ted and I to cover the office while he was out.

Again, 'yes'. I was able to contact my supervisor at DHR and tell her I wouldn't be at work Monday. She was very understanding and wished me luck in my new occupation.

I showed up at Leo's office on Monday, May 20, 1978. That day, I became a lawyer.

An accidental lawyer.

CHAPTER 8

And now, I'm a Lawyer

I never saw this coming, but it seemed like another good occupation for which I had zero experience. Leo and Barbara showed up early that morning of May 20, 1978, to welcome Ted and I to the firm, assign each of us an office, and say, "See you in two weeks."

Fortunately, Barbara's daughter was a legal secretary and knew how the office was run. Many of the things that arose during this first two weeks could simply be continued until Leo got back.

One thing that was pending and could not be put off was a trial. Ted, with no more authority than I had, assigned me the case. I had never tried a case before. I had never seen a case tried.

I got the file and started figuring it out. The case reminded me of essay questions on the bar exam. I would be representing a plaintiff who claimed he had a contract with the defendant for some kind of in-home training services. The supposed agreement was an oral contract, nothing in writing. The case was set in the Jefferson County District Court, also known as Small Claims

Court. The Judge would be the decider of facts as there are no juries in this Court.

The amount in question was under a thousand dollars and the plaintiff and defendant would be the only people to testify. I received a call prior to trial from the defendant's attorney, Charlie Waldrep. He told me that I had no case, and I should bring a 'big bat and ball' to the trial, whatever that means. I guess it's a lawyer thing.

I had gone over the case with my plaintiff, and we showed up for Court at the designated time.

The first trial I had ever seen, and I was in it. Charlie was kind to me, knowing that I was a 'baby lawyer,' a term used for an attorney with less than five years of practice, and we had several occasions to work with each other over the years.

Our parties testified, we made our argument, and the Judge found for the defendant. This was obviously the correct verdict regarding this verbal contract, but now I'm 0-1 in trials.

Finally, Leo and Barbara returned to America.

In June, I went to Montgomery with my mom and dad, Carolyn, Kevin and Ashley, for the swearing in ceremony as a member of the Bar of the State of Alabama.

In Leo's office, we had meetings once a week in the evening to go over every case in the office. He had assigned Ted and I a caseload, and these meetings were very helpful in making sure we were properly handling them. This was extremely beneficial in learning the nuances of practicing law.

Leo began taking me with him as co-counsel in jury trials. I watched and learned from this excellent trial lawyer. He was showing me how to direct and cross-examine witnesses, enter documents into evidence, make appropriate objections, and deliver opening and closing arguments. I learned much more about these elements of trial procedure than I had in law school.

I began to enjoy trial work, as Leo assigned me a greater role. Eventually, I was trying all aspects of a trial, with Leo making sure I didn't leave anything out.

When Ted and I had been with Leo for a year, he made us partners. The firm was now 'Costello, Gideon and Melton,' and our income increased over the salary we had been earning.

This was all good except for one problem. The work required sixty or more hours per week. There was no time left for extracurricular activities. It was all law, all the time. This was the life for most successful trial lawyers.

Early in my career, I came across a case from Arizona. Like Alabama, their State Bar Association prohibited a lawyer from any form of advertising. An Arizona lawyer who was penalized for violating this rule appealed it to court, and the ban on advertising was voided, with some exceptions such as comparing the advertising attorney's work with that of other lawyers. I thought, 'that's interesting, I think I'll try it.' Leo agreed to let me, so I put an ad in The Birmingham News. It was not really designed as an 'ad', but rather an 'announcement.' It read 'Michael Melton announces that he has begun practicing law' with the address and phone number of the office.

I immediately received notice from the Alabama Bar Association that I had violated the Code of Ethics regarding advertising. I wrote back, citing the Arizona case, and pointed out that this wasn't an advertisement, just an announcement. We went back and forth for months. They proposed that a hearing be scheduled for the charges. I replied that they could schedule the hearing any time convenient to them. Next, they asked if I would accept a letter of censure, and I answered 'no.' Then, after several months, they dismissed the charge altogether.

Now I feel responsible for the wall-to-wall advertising on TV by lawyers.

Leo had taken a case representing a man who was suffering from a fatal case of cancer. His doctor determined that the cancer was caused by his exposure to microwaves in the 1950s while serving in the Army. The problem with the case, the Alabama Statute of Limitations required that a civil suit must be brought within two years of the act causing the injury. The defendants, which included Raytheon and General Electric among others, filed their Summary Judgment Motions, citing that the time for the plaintiff to file suit had expired in the 1950s, or two years after he was last exposed to microwaves. In discovery, we had learned that the defendants were aware of the dangers the microwaves presented.

As a sidenote, there are four elements to pre-trial discovery in a civil case that all parties engage in; Depositions of parties and witnesses taken in person, under oath, and recorded. Interrogatories are questions submitted to the other side. A Request for Production of Documents speaks for itself. A Request for Admissions is a list of statements for the other party to answer with a yes or no. Okay, that's your free law lesson.

The Judge dismissed our lawsuit pursuant to the Statute of Limitations, ruling that under the law, plaintiff would have had to file suit many years before he even knew he had been harmed. We appealed the case to the Alabama Supreme Court and Leo asked me to write the brief.

I began by noting that the defendants were aware of the danger imposed on the plaintiff, but never warned him about it. They never took any remedial action to protect him from the danger, and probably many other soldiers suffered similar injuries.

My argument, as I set out in my Brief, was that the defendants had fired a gun at the plaintiff in the 1950s, but the bullet didn't strike him for twenty years.

The Supreme Court ruled against us 5 to 4. Four of the Justices thought our argument that the Statute should begin at the time an injured party 'knew or should have known' of the injury was correct. The majority opinion stated that our argument was valid, but that it was up to the State Legislature, rather than the Court, to make this change.

Eventually, the change was made, but much too late for our plaintiff who had passed away.

I was learning more every day from Leo, gaining more confidence in handling jury trials. I came to love the challenge and the competition.

However, that one problem continued, the number of hours necessary to do this private practice job.

The income was good, but time was more valuable.

CHAPTER 9

Why Not?

My law practice seemed much like that of other lawyers I had met that were also in private practice. The consensus opinion of these attorneys was, the more money you made, the more time you spent doing it.

I ran into a lawyer, Hampton Brown, who worked as a Public Defender with The Legal Aid Society. He told me that the pay was reasonable, although less than I was currently making, but you get to try a lot of cases. Most interesting to me, a Legal Aid lawyer generally worked only forty hours a week. And, surprise, they had an opening. So, I applied for the position.

I'm starting to see a pattern here.

It was difficult turning in a resignation to my law firm, Leo had done so much for me. He was such a kind man, and simply said to me, "I understand."

I was hired by Legal Aid, and they gave me sufficient time to catch Leo up on my cases. The Legal Aid Society offices were located only two blocks from Leo's place.

The city operated four municipal courts. Two were in city

hall, presided over by Judge Tennant Smallwood and Judge Peter Hall. Another court was in the Ensley neighborhood, upstairs from the Birmingham Police Department's West Precinct. Bill Rohr was the presiding Judge in this Court, and the docket was held in the evening. There was also a Court attached to the city jail on the south side of Birmingham, presided over by Judge Aloysius Golden.

I was assigned as the Public Defender in Judge Peter Hall's Court. Judge Hall was the first Black Municipal Court judge in Birmingham. The prosecutor in this court was Barron Lankster, working out of the city's law department.

The job was not complicated. A defendant would be called to the bench and Judge Hall would ask if they had a lawyer. If they wished to have one but couldn't afford it, he would call me up. I then completed an information form concerning employment and income to determine if they were eligible for me to represent them. I took on many clients through this process.

Most criminal courts, at any level, allow the prosecutor and defense attorney to work out a plea agreement, with a suggested penalty if the defendant admits guilt. Judge Hall did not subscribe to this procedure. In his court, if the defendant wished to plead guilty, he had to enter a 'blind plea' to the Judge, who would set the penalty.

This method resulted in many cases being set for trial. Fine with me, I loved trying cases. City courts handle only misdemeanors, felonies were handled in the circuit courts. The maximum sentence in Municipal Court was one year in jail, and five hundred dollars in fines. In trying so many cases, I significantly improved my examination and cross-examination skills.

During my time as Public Defender, approximately one year, Barron and I became good friends. On days when the afternoon docket finished early, we often went to Highland Raquet Club and played tennis.

Each morning the docket was called at 9:00am and the afternoon docket at 1:30pm. Roughly sixty cases appeared on each docket. Assault and battery cases and DUIs were the ones most often resulting in trial.

Some were semi-humorous. In one case I defended, a woman appeared before the Court charged with assault and battery by her husband. As the complainant described the attack during the trial, he testified his wife had hit him on the head with a skillet. Under questioning, they both admitted that they had been before Judge Hall two years earlier. On that occasion, the wife had also hit her husband in the head with a skillet. They further indicated that they were still together, and neither had any plans to terminate their marriage.

"I find you guilty," decreed Judge Hall to the wife. "Your sentence is a one hundred dollar fine. And lose the skillet."

During this time my dad suffered a stroke, from which he never fully recovered. After leaving the hospital, he went to the Lakeshore Rehabilitation Center. Dad received great help there, and although he could never return to work at Britling Cafeteria, he was able to function well in his job as father and grandfather.

Spending time with him at Lakeshore, I learned about volunteers who came there to work with the patients in sports, or to provide entertainment. I spoke to the lady handling this part of the rehab program and she invited me to participate. We set a couple of dates, and I held singalongs for around two dozen of the residents. I would make several copies of lyrics to popular songs, pass them out, and then play my acoustic guitar while we all sang along. James Taylor, The Eagles, Elton John, Jim Croce, and John Denver were the favorites. Worked great there, but when I took this idea to a nursing home, the residents didn't know any of these artists, and I didn't know any Frank Sinatra.

In the meantime, a Circuit Court Judgeship came open. The present Judge was retiring, and the successor would be appointed by Governor Fob James. The Jefferson County Judicial Conference, with membership consisting of judges, attorneys, and businesspeople, would interview all the applicants, and submit to the Governor the three they found most suited for the job. The Conference interviewed nineteen applicants for the judgeship and selected Barron Langster, Sandra Ross, and me.

We each went to Montgomery to be interviewed by Governor James. My interview went well, but in the end, he selected Sandra Ross for the position. She was very well qualified and did a great job on the bench.

I remember that I really wanted the judgeship at the time, but a few years later, my non-selection worked out well for me. After becoming a full-time trial lawyer, I looked at judgeships in a totally different way. Trials became a contest between me and the other lawyer. As Leo had taught me, the lawyer most prepared and who best presented their case to the jury would be the winner. In these contests, the Judge was a referee.

I was much more suited to be a player.

CHAPTER 10

Politics, Briefly

In 1981, the Birmingham City Council consisted of nine councilors, each representing a different district of the city. At that time, there were three administrative assistants serving the entire council. Today, each of the council members have their own staff of assistants.

While working in the municipal court as a Public Defender, I learned that one of the council assistants had departed and the council was going to hire a replacement. I had never been employed in a job involving politics before.

So, I applied for the position. I had no idea what an administrative assistant to the city council did. Nothing new there.

When I went before the nine councilors to be interviewed for the position, Councilman David Herring brought up my resume. He asked, "You've had a lot of jobs, why are you interested in this one?" He told me that it was time to settle down, and that I could earn more as a lawyer than a council aide. I answered, "Making a lot of money has never been my reason to take a job.

I don't know if I will ever settle down to one profession. This job might lead me to something else later."

They hired me anyway.

The Chief Administrative Assistant was Tom Fletcher. Marilyn Lewis and I were under his supervision. The job turned out to be interesting, and chaotic. Every day was different.

The three of us were constantly being called by various council members for information concerning issues they were dealing with. I was often asked to accompany a council member to meetings with constituents, or businesses working under contracts with the city. I got a lot of free dinners at these meetings.

My activities with so many of the councilors were learning experiences. Each taught a different story; why they were in politics, and what their goals were for the city. On one occasion, Bessie Estelle, one of the first Black councilors in Birmingham, asked if I would drive her to Montgomery for a meeting. I drove her down, and we had lengthy and fascinating conversations about the city's past and present.

Councilor Pete Clifford became a friend, and on one occasion invited my family to dinner at his home. Councilman William Bell later became the Mayor of Birmingham, and Jeff Germany was elected a Jefferson County Commissioner.

The most active day was Tuesday when the council had its weekly public meeting. The day began in the Council Conference Room with a pre-council meeting to go over the items scheduled for discussion that day.

The administrative assistants were charged with knowing all about every item on the agenda, answering questions about them from councilors at the pre-council meeting. That took a lot of research and study, but we were always ready.

The Council President at that time was Nina Miglionico, known as 'Ms. Nina,' I loved working with her, and we often had lunch together. Always, as she insisted, in a Birmingham restaurant.

Using my background as a lawyer, Tom would assign me to present legal issues to the Council, such as a lengthy Summary of the Affirmative Action Consent Decree setting out the parameters for future employee hirings by the City, regarding race and gender. I later submitted a summary regarding the city's compliance with this Decree.

Another issue I summarized was the city's policy regarding the Health and Benefits Board of the City.

I don't recall how it happened, but I was appointed to the Alabama March of Dimes Committee. I served a year, meeting periodically in various cities with the other board members. It was an educational experience, learning how large charitable organizations raise funds. We were able to keep its fund raising active, competing with so many other worthy causes.

While working on the City's annual budget, I interviewed the directors of each of the city departments to discuss their financial and personnel needs for the upcoming fiscal year.

One of the department heads I would be interviewing was the City Attorney, Jim Baker, who had previously been a partner in the law firm Adams, Clemon, and Baker. Each of these attorneys made history. Jim Baker was the first Black City Attorney for Birmingham, U.W. Clemon was the first appointed Black United States District Court Judge for the Northern District of Alabama, and Oscar Adams was the first Black Alabama Supreme Court Justice. My path would put me in contact with all of them in the coming years.

During these preparations for the budget hearings, I visited Mr. Baker in his office on the sixth floor of City Hall. After going over the law department's budget, he asked me about my plans. He said that Barron Langster, the prosecutor in Judge Peter Hall's Court, was leaving the law department and moving to Tuscaloosa. Barron later became the District Attorney for that county.

And then, he asked me the question that I had heard a few times before. "Would you consider coming to work in the Law Department as the prosecutor in Judge Hall's Court?"

But of course. Yes.

I had been with the City Council about six months when I advised them that I had accepted a position as Assistant City Attorney in the City's Law Department.

I had warned them when they hired me.

CHAPTER 11

Finally, a Long-term Gig

I didn't know it at the time, but I would work in the Law Department of the City of Birmingham as Assistant City Attorney and later as Principal Attorney for twenty-seven years. The job, over the years, had great challenges and rewards. I also got to participate in many extracurricular activities during my time with the city.

I began prosecuting in Judge Hall's Court and it felt like coming home, having been the Public Defender in his Court just six months earlier.

Judge Hall's Court, for many defense attorneys, was not an easy place to be. He could be quite irascible, if not antagonistic toward lawyers. Knowing him as well as I did by then, his attitude was possibly caused by the way he had been treated during his career as a Black attorney in Alabama. I knew many attorneys who would not take a case in his court for any amount of money.

Fortunately, the Judge and I got along very well. The fact that we were both veterans might have had a role in this relationship.

We talked often about our time in the service. Judge Hall had a large office behind the courtroom, and my smaller office was nearby. I would visit him each morning to discuss that day's dockets, but our conversations sometimes led to swapping war stories. Often, I would be staring at my watch, the morning docket was set for 9:00am, and we would still be talking until maybe 9:30 or 10:00 o'clock. I would suggest that maybe we should go into the courtroom and get started. His usual response was, "They'll wait."

The Judge had some great stories, and I really did enjoy our conversations. He told me about a train ride to Chicago where he was enrolled in law school. He had gotten to meet the famous singer, Lena Horne, on the train, and I could tell this chance meeting was still exciting for him.

My favorite story that he shared occurred in the early 1960s, when he was traveling around the state representing people in civil rights cases. Judge said that he didn't have access to a decent law library, just a couple of old textbooks that he would place on his courtroom table to give the impression that he had the appropriate legal references for the case at hand.

Jim Clark was the Sheriff of Dallas County, Alabama from 1955 to1966. The County seat was a town called Selma. You've probably heard of it. Sheriff Clark opposed integration and voting rights. He and his deputies had used extreme methods to prevent Black citizens from registering to vote, including baton beatings and cattle prods.

Attorney Peter Hall brought a lawsuit on behalf of several county residents against Sheriff Clark and Dallas County, claiming violation of their civil right to register and vote in elections.

At one point in the trial, Sheriff Clark was called as a witness by the defense during which he denied having used excessive force to prevent Black citizens from registering to vote. When Attorney Hall began his cross-examination, he asked Clark, "In Alabama, what is the factor used to determine if a person is Black?"

Clark responded, "Under the Alabama Constitution, if you are one-sixteenth Black, then you are Black under the law."

Peter Hall then asked the Sheriff, "Based on that, under Alabama Law, what percentage of Black are you?"

Clark's face got very red, and he leaned forward to angrily respond.

Attorney Hall, speaking to the Court, said "Your Honor, I withdraw the question. All he knows is what his mama told him, and that would be hearsay."

The courage of this Civil Rights Lawyer is beyond comprehension. Peter Hall was not afraid of anyone.

The first floor of Birmingham City Hall houses two courtrooms, separated by a large room where the City Clerk's facilities are located. There are many desks and numerous people working there. My daughter Ashley was seven years old the summer I served as prosecutor, and I would often bring her to work with me. She enjoyed it and would hang out in the courtroom or the clerk's area, where she got to know many of the workers.

One morning, after finishing the docket, I looked for Ashley so we could eat lunch before the afternoon docket. She was nowhere around, but I knew Ashley would show up momentarily to go to lunch. Exploring city hall was something else she loved to do. When Ashley came back, she handed me a polaroid picture in which she is sitting behind Mayor Arrington's desk in his office on the third floor. The mayor had welcomed her when she wandered in, took her picture, and autographed it. She still has that picture.

Trying many cases in Judge Hall's Court further enhanced my skills at witness examination. One case stands out, the way the testimony went down was epic. A young lady had sworn out warrants for Assault and Harassment against her ex-boyfriend. According to her Complaint, he lived with his sister and the sister's young son, a block away from her home. On the day of the incident in question, he came to her house, and through an open window, pointed a shotgun and threatened to shoot her. Fortunately, he didn't.

Prior to the beginning of testimony, I had asked for the 'rule', which was granted by Judge Hall. This requires that witnesses who would be testifying must remain outside of the courtroom until called to testify. The parties, of course, remain in court during the trial. The 'rule' is asserted in almost every civil and criminal trial, so witnesses can't hear other witnesses testify, and maybe adjust their testimony to conform.

In this case, the only witness other than the parties was the defendant's sister. She was asked to leave the courtroom and wait in the hall until called. After my complainant testified about the incident and how the defendant had pointed a shotgun at her, I rested.

The defense attorney, for some reason, called the defendant to the stand first. He testified that he never left his residence that day because he was taking care of his sister's son while she was at work as a nurse's assistant.

When you have handled many cross-examinations, experience teaches you how to take a witness where you want them to go.

And it worked. In my cross, I only asked two questions, "You didn't point a shotgun at her did you." "No," he replied. If a question sets forth a set of facts and is phrased as if I already know the answer to a leading question, the witness might feel the need to agree.

"You don't even own a shotgun, do you?"

"No, I don't."

No further questions from the prosecutor. The defense attorney knew exactly where I was going and declined to call the sister to testify. But I called her as a rebuttal witness. She was sworn in, and I said, "I have only one question to ask you. When you got home from work that day, was the shotgun in the same place as it was when you went to work?"

"Yes sir," she proudly responded, "It had not been moved."

No further questions.

CHAPTER 12

Moving On Up

I had been the prosecutor in Judge Hall's Court for a year when Mr. Baker asked me to come to his office. There were twenty lawyers on staff in the Law Department, each with a specific area of expertise. Some of the jobs were prosecutor, city contracts, real estate, Jefferson County Personnel Board appeals, ordinances, and civil trials.

Mr. Baker indicated that he needed another lawyer to defend the city and its employees in civil lawsuits in State and Federal Trial Courts, and Appellate Courts. He said that he had been keeping up with my trial work, and asked if I would be willing to move up to the sixth floor and work in the civil trial section of the Law Department. I would also handle the assignment of new lawsuits to the trial lawyers.

Hmm, let me think.

Yes.

I would miss my relationship with Judge Hall, but he said that he had recommended me to Mr. Baker for this new assignment.

Several years later, I was asked to come to Judge Hall's home to say goodbye to him as he passed away. He wasn't conscious, but I talked to him about our times in court. Peter Hall had a remarkable life. He was my hero and my friend.

I packed my gear and moved upstairs. There were lawyers, paralegals, and secretaries that I had never met before. I was the new kid on the block. I soon learned that they were all talented and devoted to serving the city. My office, secretary, and paralegal were assigned, and I moved in.

Once again, I'm on a learning curve in a position for which I have no prior experience. There were five lawyers in the department assigned to handle civil lawsuits. Each lawyer managed a caseload of roughly thirty-five active lawsuits. I began studying the cases I inherited, and figuring where each was in their proceedings.

In the 1980s, the most a plaintiff could recover from an Alabama municipality in civil court was one hundred thousand dollars. Personal injury lawyers were accustomed to claiming unlimited damages in their civil cases, particularly when the party sued was covered by insurance. Plaintiff lawyers did not like this limit on recovery from a city.

Some of these attorneys discovered what they thought would be a way to recover more than the maximum against the city under state law. There was a federal statute, titled 42 United States Code, section 1983, that allowed, in addition to a claim for negligence under state law, the addition of a federal civil rights claim.

This federal statute allowed a claim for damages caused by violation of civil rights due to 'a custom, policy, or practice' of a city, which caused them harm. The reason this had become a popular addition to a lawsuit, there was no limit under this statute as to how much a plaintiff could recover from a city if they could prove a civil rights violation.

Spoiler Alert – No plaintiff ever recovered against Birmingham under this statute. They never proved that the City had any custom, policy, or practice that violated civil rights.

Municipal law, under the Code of Alabama, Section 11-47-23, requires an injured party to file a claim with the City Clerk within six months of the injury. This requirement is only waived if a lawsuit was filed within that first six months. The reason for this statute was to allow a city in Alabama to take corrective action if the claim revealed a hazardous situation, and possibly reach a settlement with the injured party. If the claim was denied by the city, the plaintiff could disagree and file suit. Some plaintiffs suffered Summary Judgment on their lawsuit because they had failed to file a timely claim and were relying on the statute of limitations for their negligence suit of two years.

They weren't aware that they had to file a claim within six months.

I was.

An unexpected event happened during my time in the department. I received a call in February 1987 from Lee Majors, a disk jockey with the radio station WSGN. He told me that on Sunday evenings he was hosting a show called, 'Whatever happened to,' interviewing members of Birmingham bands from the 1960s, and playing their records. Lee invited me to come to the station to talk about The Rites of Spring, and answer questions called in by listeners.

After the show, we discussed the possibility of having a reunion concert with the bands he had been talking to on his show. With the help of Riley Bookout, my ex-roadie, we started figuring out what we needed to do. First, we contacted seven bands, including mine, to see if they would get together and work up a set. They all enthusiastically agreed to start rehearsing.

We needed advertising, so Lee and Riley handled that. We decided to make it a charity event, and I selected the Children of Slain Police Officers (COSPO) as an excellent organization for a contribution. I went to one of their board meetings to present our proposal. They liked it and agreed to help fund the ads.

Then we needed a venue. The Boutwell Auditorium was a perfect place, but it was expensive. I went to Mayor Arrington to discuss the facility. When I told him we were raising funds for COSPO, he gave me the Boutwell at no charge.

On May 8, 1987, seven bands from the sixties got to play one more time. It was amazing to see these groups I had known twenty years ago get to play for their fans, friends, and family. We raised a nice contribution for the charity and got to travel back to our teenage years for a quick visit.

One of my favorite tasks in the law department was assigning lawsuits to the trial team. I got to pick the ones for myself that looked like they would be interesting and involved the least amount of paperwork. These cases mostly dealt with subjects such as excessive force claims against police officers, accident cases involving a city vehicle, and the ever-popular trip and fall.

I immediately began trying cases in state and federal court. The more cases I tried, the more I learned about strategies to aid in defending the city and its employees. Based on this experience, I established three mandatory actions to be taken by each of our trial lawyers in every lawsuit we handled.

First, under The Rules of Civil Procedure, upon being served with a Complaint, a defendant must file an Answer within thirty days. The policy in the law department now would be that along with the Answer, we would file a Notice of Deposition for the plaintiff. By getting the plaintiff's sworn and recorded testimony immediately, they were locked down early in the case. Plus, we get their testimony before they get ours. Always helpful.

Next, I had discovered that the city had a better forum to try cases in the United States District Court for the Northern District of Alabama than in Jefferson County Circuit Court. I was particularly impressed by the formality of trials there. Questioning witnesses required the lawyer to stand at a podium rather than wander around the courtroom. Many plaintiff's lawyers were used to the latter, where they would often use physical histrionics to make a point. They could do that in state court, but not in federal court.

As I mentioned, plaintiff attorneys had discovered Section 1983, adding it to a complaint because there was no limit on recovery. Their complaints, filed in state court, focused on the state claims, but why not just throw it in? Who knows how a jury might rule? What I had learned about such a pleading was that a complaint filed in state court containing any claim under federal law could be removed by the defense to federal court. The federal court could also try state claims, even if the federal claim was later dismissed.

In other words, now they were stuck in federal court. Plaintiff lawyers did not like having their suit relocated to federal court, particularly when Section 1983 had never been a successful claim in their suits. As they picked up on my strategy, very few Section 1983 claims were being made.

A plaintiff's lawyer friend of mine, Jeffrey William Bennett, after getting caught in my trap once, put the following line in his next complaint against the city. "This Complaint specifically makes no federal claims under 42USC Section 1983, or any other federal statute."

The last rule I established was that in every case, after discovery was complete, a Summary Judgment Motion would be filed on behalf of the defendants. The reason for filing this after discovery was complete, it put the plaintiff in a position to have to respond with every single argument they intended to use at trial. They had to put it all out to avoid the possibility of their case being dismissed, even in a case where it was highly unlikely that the Court would grant the Summary Judgment Motion.

And plus, one year I had twenty Summary Judgment Motions granted, and in another year, twenty-one.

Not too shabby.

Everything in the pleading and discovery phases of a case has a filing deadline. I had seen so many lawyers on numerous occasions working very hard on the date the pleading was due. The lawyer, his secretary, and paralegal would be running between offices, law library, and copier, desperately trying to get the paperwork ready to file before the Court closed for the day.

I created a policy, but just for myself. I always set the filing date for a pleading two weeks ahead of its actual due date. My secretary and paralegal loved me for this. Zero stress.

This job was great, I loved being a trial lawyer. I would tell myself that I was a sideman in my musical life. But when I was in trial, I was the frontman. Nice.

Carolyn had taken up the hobby of running. She started by just jogging circles in the back yard. Before long, she felt ready for some competition. With friends that also ran, Carolyn began signing up for 10K runs. She eventually won dozens of trophies in these races. At the same time, Carolyn opened and operated two women's clothing stores, called 'Cute Stuff.'

In 1991, Demetrius Newton was appointed as the City Attorney when Jim Baker retired. Demetrius was also serving as an Alabama State Representative, two jobs for which he was eminently qualified. He was the first Black legislator to serve as president pro tem. He held the position of City Attorney until 1999.

During his tenure, I had a run of good trial results in state and federal court. When I had reached sixteen trial wins in a row, I began putting a sheet of paper on his chair with just the number of the win on it. The first one I put down had the number '17.' This run ended with the number '25.' Twenty-five jury trial wins in a row. I was proud of my lawyer skills.

In 1999, Tamara Harris Johnson was appointed City Attorney, taking over from Demetrius when he retired, and served until 2007.

In the U.S. District Court for the Northern District of Alabama, an appeal of an adverse ruling or verdict of a case went to the Eleventh Circuit Court of Appeals in Atlanta. I had the privilege of arguing twelve appeals before this Court, just one step below the United States Supreme Court. The side bringing the appeal is called the Appellant, the party defending the appeal is the Appellee. I was the Appellee in the twelve cases, and successful in eleven. An appellate court's ruling in my favor confirmed my win in the District Court.

I'm not remembering why I lost the one.

A couple of the appeals had interesting side lines. Charlie Wyatt went with me for my first 11th Circuit Appellate Court hearing. Charlie had argued cases before the Court a few times, and he had been my co-counsel in the trial of this case. I would be handling the argument in this one.

Unfortunately, Charlie took me on a tour of Atlanta establishments that served adult beverages, and he was buying the drinks. I was severely intoxicated by the time we got back to the hotel. And it was very late.

The next morning, Charlie had a nice breakfast, while I was trying to keep the prior day's breakfast down.

We arrived in Court about an hour before the nine o'clock docket. Several other cases were also set for that date. I found the courtroom to be quite intimidating. The justices bench seemed to be two stories high, they would be looking down on me. The podium where I would make my argument had three lights. Green meant I could start talking, yellow meant time to wrap-up, and red meant shut up.

When my case was called, I walked to the podium with my file and an empty waste can, which I placed next to me on the floor in case I should hurl. The Justices made no comment about the can, which I appreciated. I made it through without embarrassing myself.

I never took Charlie with me again.

On another occasion, I arrived in the 11th Circuit courtroom in much better shape than that time with Charlie.

I noticed there were no other cases set but mine. Just me and the appellant's attorney. No pressure. Piece of cake.

The appellant's attorney finished his presentation, and as I stood to make mine for the appellee, I heard the courtroom door open. Looking back from the podium, I observed twenty Atlanta residents, led by former Attorney General of the United States, Griffin Bell, enter the courtroom.

The Presiding Justice stated that the group was there for an emergency hearing and would be heard after my case.

So, now I'm arguing my case in front of Griffin Bell and twenty people I don't know. I remember struggling for a couple of minutes. I knew I was talking, just not sure what I was saying. I made it through and got to shake hands with a former Attorney General.

I'm going to talk about some of my more interesting trials, but first I want to tell you about some extracurricular activities I participated in while working for the City of Birmingham. I always got approval from my boss first, affirming that it wouldn't interfere with my city job. They did not interfere at all.

If this is going to be a memoir, seems like it should have the bad as well as the good. I don't know where to properly put this in the book, so this is as good a place as any.

Like Bruce Springsteen said in his song, "like a river that don't know where it's flowing, I took a wrong turn and I just kept going."

In 1989, Carolyn and I got divorced. My words can't make it right.

CHAPTER 13

Taekwondo and Softball

In 1984, Ashley, nine years old, asked me if she could take lessons in taekwondo. She had a friend who was taking the course and it sounded like fun. We went to the Craig Collars dojo in Centerpoint and I signed us both up for the course.

I mean, why not? Craig Collars operated several locations in the Birmingham area. He was a sixth-degree black belt in the art. Only black belts higher than sixth degree could test him for promotion, and there were none in the U.S. He had to go to Korea to find higher black belt degrees to test him for seventh degree, which he did.

A good friend of mine, David Broome, was one of the first-degree black belt instructors at this dojo. We had been friends since the 1960s, when we were both playing in rock bands. He was the talented keyboardist for a band called The Individuals. We had gone fishing together more times than I can count.

Classes were taught three evenings a week, and Saturday morning.

Ashley, after a few lessons, decided that this wasn't for her.

I stayed with it for four and a half years, working my way from white belt, to yellow, green, blue, red, and ultimately, black belt. Training was a great exercise and confidence builder, which are the goals of taekwondo. I particularly liked the basic tenet of the discipline, taekwondo is a defensive, not an offensive art.

I got to compete in a National Taekwondo Tournament held in Birmingham when I was at the red belt level. Fortunately, the competition was divided into groups by age. I scored a Third Place in sparring and got a nice trophy.

Testing for black belt was very intense, many difficult skills to master and then perform in front of a panel of black belts and Craig Collars. After passing each test to move up to a higher color belt, I was ready to take the test for black belt. This test involved what is termed a 'form,' containing sixty-five different kicks, punches, and blocks in a prescribed order. Then the second part, sparring with a black belt. Finally, the last segment required breaking wood with a hand technique and a foot technique. I passed, I was awarded a black belt, and I left the sport.

Mission accomplished.

When Ashley was thirteen, she took up softball, to join many of her friends in the sport. They had been playing for a few years, but this was Ashley's first time. I volunteered to be an assistant coach, watching her as she became better at fielding and batting. The coach put her in center field to gain experience, and this became her permanent position.

The team picked the name 'Stingers,' and their trademark was fixing each other's hair with a 'French braid' before each game. As a team, they were very good. After each game, we took the team to the local Taco Bell, a treat they loved.

That year, the Stingers won enough games to play for the

League Championship. The team they would be playing had one more win than the Stingers. The way it worked, the other team only had to win one game, but the Stingers had to beat them twice to earn the Championship.

It started well. The Stingers won the first game. Now, shortly after the first game, they had to beat this same team one more time.

The League's games had seven innings. This last game was close, the Stingers batted the top of the seventh and were one run ahead. At the bottom of the seventh, the opponents had runners on first and second base, with one out. Ashley was playing deep in center field, her team hoping to keep their opponent from scoring with the two base runners and winning the championship.

The next batter hit a long, high ball toward center field. The ball was coming down well in front of Ashley, and she began running toward where it would land. The runners had already started around the bases, and it appeared that this would be the last play of the game.

Ashley had a different plan. She ran fast enough to catch the fly ball. Out two. Then, like a pro, she threw the ball to the second base player. Out three. Game over. Championship to the Stingers.

And the team carried Ashley off the field.

My dad set this up

Pop Warner football player

Varsity tennis player and Ronnie

Bass guitar, The Rites of Spring

Signing autographs after a show

Poster for a concert in Georgia

USAF souvenirs

The paperwork

A Taekwondo black belt

Catfish Studio

Closing Argument

CHAPTER 14

Acting Out

Riley Bookout, as I mentioned earlier, had been a roadie in my 1960's band, The Rites of Spring. I guess we were kind of related, my brother Ronnie was married to his sister, Sally. Sometime in the late 1980s, he was involved with a theater group named ACTA. I don't know what those letters stand for, but I know it was in Trussville, Alabama and had a nice theater for the plays it presented.

Riley was contributing his skills to ACTA as a set designer and builder. He told me that ACTA was taking auditions for an upcoming musical, 'Annie Get Your Gun,' and suggested that I try out for a role. You probably know what I did.

Theater was something I had never tried before, but it sounded interesting. I auditioned and was selected for the role of Mac, an assistant to one of the lead characters, Buffalo Bill.

I was amazed by the amount of time spent rehearsing, and how close I became to the other cast members. They were veterans in theater performances, and I learned a lot about what a cast goes through preparing a play for presentation. With the numerous rehearsals came a confidence that I could do this. I was ready.

The musical had thirty-five cast members, ten of whom were children. They were as talented and seasoned as the adult actors. In addition, there were four complete stage settings, keeping Riley and his crew busy. The Director and Choreographer was Mary Lynne Robbins, and the music was provided by Gayle Glenn on piano. They were both professionals, and great to work with.

The stage was very deep, and behind it was a large room for cast members to wait their cue. The room also had several shelves, each marked with an act and scene number, where the props were stored. A prop manager made sure they arrived on stage at the appropriate time.

We were scheduled to perform the musical six times, and all the shows were sold out.

Showtime.

Everyone hit their mark and we were underway, three hours per show. We were kicking it and having a wonderful time. The kids in the cast played their parts with enthusiasm, and the audience seemed to be having as much fun as we were.

In addition to my lines, I got to do a song and dance to 'My Defenses are Down.' I am not a dancer, so they dumbed it down for me. Later I joined an ensemble for the song 'There's No Business like Show Business.'

Then the last show was over, and we had a cast party. The play had been filmed and each cast member received a DVD. We made our good-byes to friends we would probably never see again but had shared a moment as family.

I auditioned one more time with ACTA and got a role in

the play "Pillow Talk.' This was not a musical and had a much smaller cast. The comedy was much more laid back than 'Annie,' but still fun.

And that was the end of my acting career.

CHAPTER 15

Fire By Night

Naturally, something unexpected came up soon after my brief foray in the theater. It was 1993, and I got a phone call from Richard Hutto. Richard was familiar with my background as a bass player and had seen The Rites of Spring in concert in the 1960s.

He told me that he was the sound and light man for a contemporary Christian rock band called 'Fire by Night,' based at the First Baptist Church in Trussville. The band's bass player had moved to Atlanta, and they were looking for a replacement. I agreed to audition and met the members of the band. They ranged in age from twenty-one to thirty-two. I was forty-two at the time, and after playing a few tunes, they huddled and then asked me to join the band. They were very talented songwriters and musicians.

Casey Jones played keyboards, harmonica, and vocals. Tim Forehand played lead guitar and vocals. Eddie Joe Powell played lead and slide guitar. Bryan Hammond, the twenty-one-year-old, was the drummer.

And now, I'm on bass and vocals with an amazing band I had never heard of. I immediately began playing with them after the audition. Every Wednesday evening, the band played in the church's large recreation center before an audience of six hundred teenagers. The kids loved and supported this band. I was really enjoying playing with these musicians, whose repertoire was all original music written by Casey and Tim. I got to write my own bass lines for the songs. Very satisfying for a bass player.

Our rehearsals were held on Mondays, and on the weekends, we were a traveling band. We would meet at the church on Friday, along with some volunteer roadies, to load out. There was so much equipment that a truck the size of an eighteen-wheeler was necessary to carry it all. We covered the Southeast, playing to packed audiences of teens. On one occasion, we played a Summer Youth Retreat in Fort Walton, Florida, performing twice a day for two weeks under a giant tent.

I had just met Linda Andrews on a blind date. She was the Director of the Hoover Public Library and had built it to such a level that on one occasion it was ranked the fourth best library in the country by an industry publication. It has a delicatessen, the Southern Voices writers conference, and a two hundred and fifty seat, state-of-the-art theater with regular plays and musical groups performing. And a lot of books.

Later, I'm going to tell you about some of the fascinating people I got to meet through music and/or Linda.

Okay, I've got to get back on track.

After the band finished the two-week gig, loaded out, and headed back to Trussville. I stayed behind, and Linda picked me up and we drove down the coast to St. George's Island. Two days later, there was a knock on the door, and some guy asked,

"Why are you still here? The hurricane is going to hit within an hour!" So, we packed in about three minutes and headed out.

Linda began to attend our shows and became a de facto roadie, learning to wrap the miles of cords we used and put them in the giant box on wheels called the 'coffin.'

Fire by Night recorded an album of original music at Bates Brothers Recording Studio in Pleasant Grove, Alabama. The sessions went very well. The Bates Brothers, who owned and operated the studio, were also former traveling musicians, and were very helpful in producing the tracks.

This was my first experience in a digital recording studio. I was used to analog systems where the music was recorded to tape. Boutwell, Fame, Cameo-Parkway were all analog, which meant that the entire band had to record at the same time. If one musician messed up, the whole song had to re-start. With digital, one instrument at a time could be recorded, and if necessary repaired quickly. Much more efficient. I know that some professional musicians don't like digital because they think it loses the spontaneity of the group playing together. I tend to disagree, it's at least as good, and much less stressful. Many studios now have both set-ups though, allowing a band to choose its favorite.

Fire by Night had t-shirts made to go with the recording, which was on cassette tape during this era, for merchandise to sell at our shows. Called 'merch' in the biz.

I am, of course, still a trial lawyer for the City of Birmingham at that time. On one occasion, I had a trial in Circuit Court that lasted from Monday to late Friday evening. The band was playing in Orlando, Florida on Saturday night. I wasn't available to load out on Friday and was still in Court when the band pulled out at 7:00pm.

I remember the plaintiff's attorney in this trial was Houston Brown, and the jury had been out for hours without a verdict. Around 7:30, the Judge called Houston and I back to his office, where he informed us that the jury was hopelessly deadlocked, with a count of eleven to one. If he declared a mistrial, the entire case would have to be tried again. The Judge then made a proposal; we could accept the decision of the eleven jurors that agreed, without letting us know whether they were for the plaintiff or defendant. Houston said that he would accept that, but on this occasion, my answer was 'no.' How odd of me. As I told Houston and the Judge, I am not a gambler, although my work history belies that statement. But I could not settle the case on the flip of a coin. The Judge declared a mistrial, and the case was reset for trial.

And, by-the-way, the Judge later told me that the eleven jurors voted for my side. Oh well.

Fire by Night had an incredible inventory of stage equipment, things that weren't even available to bands like mine in the 1960s. We each had a monitor so we could hear the whole band. My bass amp, a Peavey combo, had a direct box which allowed my bass volume to be set correctly by Richard, the sound man. His very large board was set up at the back of the venue where he created the mix for instruments and vocals. My amp was just a monitor for me, while my bass line was coming through the four big main speakers. Richard, at the same time, was controlling our power boosters, lights and smoke devices. We were very loud.

Bryan's drums had a large, raised platform, surrounded by a three-piece plexiglass shield. He had two monitors in his 'cage,' and a sign on the shield that read 'Do Not Feed the Drummer.'

Around 1995, the band dissolved. Tim was an ordained Baptist minister and Youth Director at another church. Tim and Casey concluded that we had become too commercial, getting paid for the shows and selling merchandise.

I understood their concerns. It had been a great experience playing with these talented musicians though. I became a better bass player during those three years.

And, I thought, who knows what might happen next.

CHAPTER 16

The Alabama Troubadours

Sometime in 1998, I received a phone call from Karren Pell, a Nashville singer-songwriter. She was putting together a band to travel on weekends playing her original songs. The first shows would be in the Hoover Library Theater based on an arrangement she made with the Director, Linda Andrews. Linda had helped promote the project with Karren and provided a grant to get it started. Karren knew from talking to Linda that I played bass and asked if I would like to audition.

I told her 'No.'

Just kidding. She set up an appointment with her representative and I drove to Nashville to meet him at his home. I set up in his living room and played a few lines to recordings by Karren that I had never heard before. I was used to this; it just takes a second or two to find the key and chord progression. Then I told him about my prior experience. I had played blues, R&B, and rock, but not Americana, which was Karren's genre.

Then he said, "You'll do. The only way I want to notice you is if you quit playing."

I said, "I can do that."

Once again, I'm back in the music business, and I met the band. Karren sang lead and played rhythm guitar. Her husband, Tim Henderson, played lead on guitar, mandolin, and violin. Matina Johnson, a twenty-one-year-old young lady, sang harmony and played the recorder, an instrument like a flute. It would be just the four of us, no drummer, so I was the rhythm section. I loved the way Karren introduced me at shows. "On bass guitar, Mighty Michael Melton, laying down that firm foundation." Super cool.

There was a massive difference between this band and my last gig. Instead of an eighteen-wheeler to haul our gear, we could put it all in the trunks of our cars. I was still using my Yamaha BX-1 bass and Peavey amp from my days with Fire by Night, I just didn't have to crank it up to ten.

For this project, Karren had written songs that would define the band's name, The Alabama Troubadours. Each song dealt with an out-of-the-way place in the State of Alabama; the Coon Dog Cemetery, Moundville, Bon Secour, Old Cahaba, Tallassee, Brother Joseph's Wayside Shrine, The Boll Weevil Statue, Mentone and many more. Each song captured the essence of its subject's location. They were very good, and plus, once again, I got to write my bass lines.

In addition, a well-known photographer and Instructor at the University of Alabama, Chip Cooper, created a large, representative photo of each of the sites the songs described, and we displayed them on easels when we performed.

Over the next ten years, we played many shows, mostly at colleges and music festivals. A few of them stand out because they were played in unusual locations.

There is a building in downtown Birmingham that is set up for large meetings. We got booked to play during lunch there for a gathering of local lawyers and judges. I got the strangest looks from many of them I knew from my lawyering job. It looked like they were trying to figure out if I was the lawyer they knew, or just a similar looking bass player.

During a Writer's Conference in Nashville, we set up and played on the front steps of the State Capitol of Tennessee. And then, coincidentally, we played on the Quad in Tuscaloosa before an Alabama vs. Tennessee football game.

The most unusual show we ever played was at The Birmingham Fairgrounds for two nights at the Alabama State Fair,

in the beer tent,

next to the roller coaster,

following an Elvis impersonator.

It doesn't get any weirder than that. But I got to sing a solo, Willie Nelson's 'Blue Eyes Crying in the Rain.' Kevin was there, helping Erik Kontzen video the show.

My favorite performance with the group was not as the Troubadours and had none of the songs the group had been playing over the years.

The Alabama Shakespeare Festival Theater in Montgomery is a very well-regarded venue for plays.

The theater was producing a one woman play and someone, I don't think it was Shakespeare, contacted Karren about providing the music. Karren accepted the challenge and she and Tim wrote four songs, one to introduce each Act. Tim and Karren had moved from Nashville to Montgomery. Tim had a Ph.D. in history, had written books on the subject, and was now teaching at the Montgomery campus of Auburn University. Then Karren decided to become a professor. She earned a master's degree and began teaching.

The play that we would be providing the music for told the story of a woman with breast cancer and the four stages she went through: discovery, treatment, the effects on her life, and recovery. It was titled, 'When Life Doesn't Turn Out the Way You Planned.' Karren could very well relate to the story.

I drove to Montgomery many times to rehearse these new songs in the theater. Our set-up was at the back of the stage behind a black scrim. We weren't visible to the audience until we started each song, and our back lighting was turned on. The play was very emotional, and from where I was sitting, I could see that there was not a dry eye in the room.

We did three performances of the play, and after the last show, we had the cast party in a local Sushi restaurant. That's where I learned that the little piece of green stuff on the plate is not chewing gum.

At some point during our journey, we decided to record a CD. Karren, a Nashville veteran, decided that we would use Vortex Studio and scheduled us to record on four consecutive Saturdays. During this time, Karren had been diagnosed with breast cancer and was receiving treatment. This did not slow her down. She made every session, and the CD was excellent.

On one of our trips to Nashville, we pulled over on I-65 near the Welcome to Alabama sign and a field of flowers. Linda, our Honorary Manager, took several pictures, one of which was used for the CD cover. Karren is wearing a big, brimmed straw hat.

My grandson William attended his first concert in

Montgomery in 2004. The band was The Troubadours, and he was eight months old. I'm sure he enjoyed the show.

I retired from the road in 2008, as well as my lawyer and teacher jobs.

In 2018, Linda invited us to have a reunion concert in the Library Theater, two shows. We got together several times to get back up to speed. At the rehearsals, we reminisced about old times.

We set up in the Theater and played our last two shows. William was in attendance, age fourteen this time. Both nights, he came onstage to sing back-up. Then he sat with us after the show at the signing table, autographing our CDs.

We received a few awards during our time together. Tallassee's Mayor gave us a Key to the city. Governor Siegelman awarded the band a 'Certificate of Appreciation to the Alabama Troubadours for their Contribution to the Arts in Alabama.'

But the biggest reward was the ten years I got to spend making music with Karren, Tim, and Matina.

CHAPTER 17

Catfish Studio

In 2003, Linda and I moved into a home in McCalla, Alabama. The house was located on a lake full of catfish, bream, crappie, and bass. We bought a small boat, and I spent hours pursuing one of my favorite pass-times, fishing.

The house had a large room upstairs and I decided to turn it into a recording studio. I had recorded in several studios in my musical career: Boutwell Studio and Bates Brothers Studio in Birmingham, Fame Studio in Muscle Shoals, Alabama, Vortex Studio in Nashville, and Cameo-Parkway Studios in Philadelphia. During those sessions I learned how a studio works, the tasks of the producer, engineer, and the band being recorded. All these pieces must come together to get the music arranged, recorded, mixed, and mastered. Then, the exciting part, listening to the result through the studio's powered speakers. Awesome.

I did a lot of research on recording decks available at the time and selected the Boss BR1600. This deck was made by the Roland Company, a very respected manufacturer of recording equipment, as well as keyboards and amplifiers.

Twenty year later, the deck is still working perfectly, and I have recorded over two hundred songs. There are many things this deck will do that still amaze me. If I don't want to put a microphone on an amplifier, I can plug a guitar directly into the deck and select from sixty different effects. Forty effects for a bass, and thirty for vocals. A vocal toolbox lets me adjust pitch, and if a small part of an instrumental or vocal needs correction, the deck lets me 'punch-in and punch-out,' recording only the correction seamlessly. And on and on.

Once a song, or group of songs is mixed and mastered, I can download it to a computer or directly to a blank CD. The quality of the recording is excellent.

My idea for the studio was to provide a place where musicians could get a good recording without having to go to an expensive professional studio. I set three requirements for its use. The potential musician must have some talent, I would only do one project at a time, and the recording was free.

I had a couple of electric, acoustic, and bass guitars, but I needed several other items: powered speakers, a drum kit, a keyboard, and condenser and dynamic microphones.

A condenser mic is 'phantom powered,' which, as I like to describe it, 'can pick up a gnat fart at forty feet.' This gives great clarity, particularly with vocals. A dynamic mic is very different, it only picks up sound very close to it. These mics are used by singers in live performances because they don't pick up every other instrument on stage. They are also useful in a studio to record drums and other percussion.

I have a friend, Gary Asher, a professional drummer and past manager of Nuncie's Music Store. I met him at Nuncie's one day to check out their drum kits and get his advice on which would be a good buy. He had a better idea. This drummer is known worldwide for owning the world's largest private collection of drums. Gary said, "Meet me tomorrow at noon in the parking lot." I met him and when he opened the van's door, there sat a four piece, 1969 vintage, blue pearl Ludwig drum kit. Just like Ringo's. You know, the Beatle?

He charged me Seven Hundred Dollars for the kit, but suggested I might want to insure it for Ten Thousand Dollars.

What a bargain, and what a friend.

I put four dynamic mics on the drums and two overhead condensers on the cymbals. This configuration worked great when recording the drums. I added a Yamaha electric keyboard and was ready to record. Then I began studying the manual for the deck and testing it out. I still don't know how to use some of its features, but what I do know is more than enough.

It seems none of the companies that were selling these types of decks are still making them. Home studios now are computer software products, 'Pro Tools,' with more tricks than my deck. In fact, this is the system William uses to create his incredible music. But Pro Tools doesn't interest me. There's nothing like having a deck with real faders, switches, and dials. It has sixteen tracks, each with sixteen virtual tracks. The Pro Tools software is much more complicated.

Plus, I'm old.

During the process of figuring out how to work the deck, I learned how to make a complete recording by myself. I would pick a song I liked, write out the lyric, and then figure out the chord progression. Some that I recorded then were, 'Bobbie McGee,' 'Cripple Creek,' and 'Maggie Mae.' I would put down a rhythm guitar first, using a click track to keep it on course.

Next were the drums. I had a foot switch to start the deck from the throne. That's what they call the drummer's seat, I don't know why. Anyway, I would listen to the guitar track through headphones, and put down the drum tracks. Then the bass, easy. I spent considerable time figuring out the lead guitar parts before recording them. If I needed keyboards, my brother Ronnie was always available. And lastly, I recorded the lead and background vocals.

Mixing is creative. I get to add any effects I want, like maybe some reverb on the guitar, and pan all the parts from left to right. After getting the mix set, I bounce all the tracks to a stereo track. Finally, I have twenty-five pre-set and adjustable mastering programs.

The moment of truth – playing it back over the powered speakers. Amazing, they all turned out well.

My daughter, Emmy Andrews, and her husband Eric Heinemann, live in Bend, Oregon. When she is planning a visit, we pick a song she would like to record, and figure out what key we'll record it in. Before she arrives, I put all the tracks down, and then when she gets in, we add her vocals. She has a great voice; we've recorded twenty songs this way over the years. My favorites are 'Landslide,' and 'Crazy Little Thing Called Love.'

The whole family, children and grandchildren, have recorded songs for Christmas.

Then, somehow, word of the studio got around, and I started getting calls from musicians asking for a session. The time I spent recording was more exciting and rewarding than I had ever expected.

One band, called 'Skin Deep,' was a five-piece group of accomplished rock musicians playing original material. We recorded an eight song CD; I gave them the master and they had it pressed with a great cover. They were all fifteen years old.

Mike Fliegel is a lawyer friend that worked with me in the city's law department. His daughter, Laura, and her friend Emma were talented musicians and songwriters. They both played guitar and keyboards, had terrific harmony vocals, and had written very good songs. They let me add bass and drums to their recording. They were just fifteen, too.

Somewhere in there, a good friend from high school, John Somerset, called and asked if I would be interested in recording a CD for the Warblers, a four-part harmony do-wop group. No problem!

Well, one problem. There were twelve singers. Each needed headphones and a device to plug them into. Got it. The hardest part in these recordings was getting them to stay in one place so their headphone cords didn't get all tangled up. Talk about herding cats.

These guys were perfectionists, and even without any instruments, just voices, recording them was very time consuming. It must have been fun though. A few years later I recorded their next CD.

That's the way the studio ran, too many recordings to recall them all, but each one unique. I know I enjoyed the process, still do. Recently I was contacted by Michael Gunnels, the singer and songwriter in my 1960's band, The Rites of Spring. He is still living and performing in Nashville, as well as writing songs to demo and sell. He has come down several times to record a good demo, twelve so far.

I also see Mike Pair, rhythm guitarist in that band, for lunch frequently. Mike and I recently contacted Dailey Vandegriff, our drummer in The Rites of Spring. We hadn't seen him since our reunion concert in 1987. I reminded him how much he cost us in drumsticks. Dailey had always insisted that we purchase sticks with his signature embossed on them. He had gotten in the habit of giving them away at shows. To girls, of course. We told him he couldn't give them away anymore. He asked if it was okay to give a stick away should it get broken, and we gave him a reluctant okay. Dailey knew exactly how to hit a rimshot that would break a stick. I believe he averaged about four breakages a night.

Just being together, brothers of the road, takes us back to our teenage years, traveling the country playing rock and roll.

There are a few changes in the studio now. We moved to Hoover, Alabama in 2012. The studio here is twice the size of the one in McCalla, so it had to be filled up. I now have an additional six-piece Ludwig kit, Hammond organ, Roland keyboard, seven amps, bigger speakers, and a pool table. My grandkids love hanging out in the studio, it's worth having it just for them. My son Kevin is an artist, creating beautiful artwork in wood. There are several pieces of his work in the house and studio, all amazing.

And I now have forty-eight electric, acoustic, and bass guitars. I believe that's enough. Probably.

CHAPTER 18

Teacher Man

One year, the Southern Voices Writer's Conference at the Hoover Public Library hosted Irish author and Pulitzer Prize winner Frank McCourt as the keynote speaker. He had written *Angela's Ashes*, *Tis*, and *Teacher Man*. Linda and I got to take Frank and his wife to dinner, a memorable evening. As you may have noticed, I borrowed his book title for this chapter. I know he won't mind, I paid for dinner.

I soon found myself in another occupation I had never considered before.

Teaching. This also qualifies as accidental.

A neighbor across the street was a professor at Jefferson State Junior College. He came over one day shortly after we moved in and asked if I would be interested in teaching a class in Criminal Procedure.

Don't make me say my answer, you know what it was.

The class met on Tuesday and Thursday evenings from 6:30 to 8:30. It was a very large class. Many of the students were preparing for careers in law enforcement, and some were already so employed.

I discovered early that I really liked teaching. The students were interested in the subject, and I was able to relate stories about some of my jury trials that were relevant to the topic.

The class and I had to negotiate a settlement of one issue though. There was a popular TV show on Tuesdays called 'The A Team,' which these tuition paying students could not afford to miss. By popular demand, we changed the Tuesday class starting time from 6:30pm to 5:30pm. This made me a very popular teacher.

I taught the course for two years, then other opportunities came up, but I learned a lot about teaching. It's not as easy as at looks, but twice as much fun.

After class one evening, a student, Steve Taylor, came up and asked if he could talk to me about a problem he was having with his dad. Steve was twenty-one years old and living at home. He told me about the situation that was causing friction between them. I talked with him awhile and he seemed satisfied with my suggestions. At the next class, Steve told me that he and his dad had worked out their disagreement and invited me to come fishing on Emerald Lake where his family lived. I got to know his mom and dad, good folks. We fished there often and remained friends until he passed away several years later.

My next teaching job was basically the same subject as the one at Jefferson State, but in a different venue. I had gotten to know the Chief of Police, Arthur V. Deutcsh, representing him in several lawsuits brought against him by his troops. He was a former New York City precinct captain that had been hired by Mayor Arrington. Many of the officers did not like him, they felt that the new chief should have been someone from the force. Chief Deutcsh did not do much to ingratiate himself with the rank and file. He took questionable disciplinary action against many of them, resulting in these suits against him. We won the suits, which did not make the officers any happier. But that was life in the Birmingham Police Department in the Deutcsh era.

The Police Academy trains recruits for duty. The school facility for classroom work is located on the south side of Birmingham. Firearm training is given at the Firing Range in east Birmingham.

Chief Deutcsh asked me to teach a course in Criminal Procedure to the rookie classes at the Academy. It sounded good, I could help them learn how to handle some of the legal situations that could arise during their career.

But first, I had to become a Certified Police Academy Instructor with the State of Alabama. I got certified and was scheduled for the next class of recruits.

I kind of tweaked the criminal procedure course I would be teaching. The course had never been taught this way before, mainly because I made it up myself.

Based on experience, I described to the recruits the best ways to relate favorably to a jury in civil cases. This included how to dress, what jewelry not to wear, how to handle cross-examination, and the advantage of having their spouse in the courtroom.

A trial begins with jury selection. Usually, a panel of thirty-six potential jurors are brought into the courtroom. They are then questioned by the Judge, plaintiff's attorney and defendant's attorney, to find twelve jurors who could listen to the evidence and render a fair and impartial verdict. This procedure is called 'voir dire,' Latin for 'to see, to hear.' Each side then has a set number of strikes to get down to the final twelve.

A common element of the voir dire is asking the panel if any of them know or are related to any of the parties or attorneys. If I was representing a police officer, I would ask him to bring his spouse to court and ask her to sit in the audience section of the courtroom. During voir dire, I would ask her to stand up, and ask the panel if any of them knew her. I wasn't really interested in their answer, the purpose was to identify the officer as a family man.

In one trial, I asked the officer's wife to stand up. She was obviously pregnant. The jury returned a verdict for the officer. I'm sure that was not the only reason for the verdict, but it didn't hurt. A year or so later, the same officer was a named defendant in another civil suit, and he came to my office to discuss strategy for the trial. I asked if he could bring his wife to court with him again. He said, "Yes, she can come, but we're not going to have another baby just for this trial."

Good enough.

Experience is the best teacher. I think I say that a lot. Probably obvious anyway, I'll try not to say it again.

While making the closing argument in a trial defending a police officer, an idea came to me out the blue the first time I used it. This new strategy seemed to work well, so it became a standard part of my closing when representing an officer. Plaintiff attorneys would say, "You're not going to use that 'Columbo' closing, are you?" or, "You're not going to deputize the jury again, are you?"

This is how it worked. I would do my usual closing, discussing the testimony and documents the jury had heard.

Then, "And so, ladies and gentlemen, the evidence clearly shows you should return a verdict for the defendant." I would turn as if to walk back to my table, pause, then turn back to the podium as if something had just occurred to me, and say: "You know, I was just thinking about something. I get up in the morning, put on my suit and tie, like many people do, and go to work. Sometimes, I'll work a little overtime, and my family might wonder if I'm going to be late for supper."

Then, pointing to the officer, I say, "This man gets up in the morning, puts on a blue uniform, a badge, and a gun. His family doesn't wonder if he will be late for supper. They wonder if he will be home at all." The jury will look at the officer, and his wife in the audience.

Verdict for the defense. Usually.

The reason this closing was effective, it was true. During my time with the city, I attended four funerals for officers killed in the line of duty.

I think this information was helpful for these rookies I was teaching at the Academy. And I did cover some criminal procedure like I was supposed to.

CHAPTER 19

More Teaching

I had occasion to try a case that involved a suit against Birmingham arising out of an incident in the city jail. An inmate was attacked by another inmate, and the injured party sued, claiming negligence on the city's part in monitoring inmate activity in the jail. I retained Raymond O. Sumrall, Ph.D., as my expert witness to testify about municipal liability arising from its jail policies and procedures. He was employed by the University of Alabama at Tuscaloosa as a professor. Dr. Sumrall gave testimony about the appropriate policies a jail should have regarding inmate-on-inmate assaults.

Dr. Sumrall related the jail's record over the prior year, 1994. The facility had handled 23,000 inmates, had a daily population of four hundred, and there had only been twenty-two assaults by prisoner on prisoner that year. He testified that this was better than any other municipal jail he was aware of. He also pointed out that generally, in any jail, there would be violent inmates. After all, it's a jail. Dr. Sumrall's testimony helped me win the trial.

After the trial was over, he invited me to be a guest lecturer in his master's class at the University to speak on constitutional rights claims brought against public entities and its employees.

It's kind of complicated, with a lot of federal case law on this area of the law. But I had been involved with this subject for years in state and federal court trials. The students in this class were great, they had also studied the topic, and the class became more of a conversation than a lecture. I got to do this twice.

One of my classmates in law school was Tom Leonard. Tom was a state representative at the time. We became friends and stayed in contact. He became a staff attorney with the University of Alabama at Birmingham, and additionally, was the Dean of the Birmingham School of Law, replacing the retired Hugh Locke, Jr. Tom called me one day and asked if I would be interested in teaching Constitutional Law on Tuesday nights.

My alma mater was calling me home. How could I possibly say no?

The school had changed locations, moving from the Jefferson County Courthouse to the Frank-Nelson Building, a few blocks away. These new facilities were nice but didn't have the majesty of the courthouse, where I would have been teaching from a judge's bench.

Alas.

I taught there for several years. The best thing about this job, later I got to work with my former students, and even competed against some of them in court.

Every practicing attorney in Alabama is required to accrue

twelve hours of Continuing Legal Education (CLE) every year. Somewhat annoying, partially because it's sometimes difficult to schedule courses relative to your area of practice. The seminars are sponsored across the state by legal organizations, and by private, for-profit companies.

Each seminar counts for three CLE hours, so to earn the twelve hours required, a lawyer must make four seminars. Check my math on that.

I learned something interesting about attorneys that presented seminars. They received six CLE hours. Soon after I discovered this shortcut, I contacted seminar providers to apply for a presentership. I made that word up.

One of the providers, Lorman Education Services, retained my services. They assigned me topics like 'Civil Liability and Law Enforcement in Alabama' and 'Police Liability in Alabama.' Not only was I getting six CLE hours for each seminar, I was also getting paid for it.

Another resource was the Alabama Association of Municipal Attorneys, where I spoke on 'The Americans with Disabilities Act and Public Facilities.'

On one occasion, I presented a paper to the Alabama League of Municipalities Midyear Law Conference at the Hilton Garden Hotel in Orange Beach, Alabama. They also paid for my hotel room, which was nice. Never made it to the beach though.

Next, I was selected to teach a seminar at the Municipal Law Conference in Huntsville on the Americans with Disabilities Act and Public Facilities. Later, I'll tell you why I knew so much about the ADA.

Once this started rolling, I never attended another seminar other than as a presenter. An additional benefit, I presented some seminars several times, just in different areas of the state, so very little preparation was necessary. I was doing at least four a year, but that was alright.

Like I said, I was getting paid.

CHAPTER 20

And Yet, More Teaching

One teaching experience I had was a little different. There is an entity titled, 'Trial Advocacy Board, Center for Advocacy and Clinical Education.' This national organization sponsors moot court competition between law schools.

Like football, but without helmets.

The Cumberland Law School, situated at Samford University in Birmingham, has always scored well at these events.

Paul Warren, the Cumberland Law School Director, asked me to serve as judge in one of the law school's Herbert W. Peterson Senior Moot Court competitions to determine which team would represent the school in the next national competition. I had tried many jury trials in state and federal court and felt confident that I could handle a fake judge role.

Cumberland Law School is a nationally recognized and accredited school. The Birmingham School of Law is not. To be accredited, a law school must have a campus and full-time professors. My law school had neither. Our campus was the

Jefferson County courthouse, and our professors were practicing lawyers, teaching part-time in the evenings.

On the upside, a graduate of my school was allowed to take the Alabama bar exam, and if passed would be authorized to practice law in Alabama. Just not in any other state. And my law school was infinitely cheaper to attend.

During my career as a lawyer, I met many judges and successful lawyers who had attended the Birmingham School of Law. They were as good as the lawyers that had graduated from those fancy accredited law schools.

The case for trial in this mock court competition that I would be judging involved a murder charge and came under the Federal Rules of Evidence and Criminal Procedure. That meant I would be playing a United States District Court Judge. The best part, I got to wear a robe and sit at the bench in the school's courtroom. Even though this was a mock trial, it was fascinating to see a trial from the perspective of a judge. I got to say things like 'denied' and 'overruled,' and 'sustained,' and then explain to the students the reasoning behind my rulings. I discovered that I knew more than I thought I did.

I was invited back two more times.

There are ninety-nine neighborhoods in Birmingham, each with an elected set of officers. The officers' mission is to speak for their neighborhoods, usually before the city's Department of Community Development, and to apply for benefits through the Birmingham Citizens Participation Program. The director of this program was Faye Dixon, and she scheduled me on several occasions to make a presentation at a neighborhood meeting. My task was to provide them with information about resources available to their neighborhood, such as federal grants, and how to apply for them.

I was able to assist the East Lake neighborhood in securing a grant, which was rewarding because that was where I grew up. Their meetings were held in the East Lake Library, where I had spent countless hours as a kid.

In 1993, the city held its annual Neighborhood Conference at the Civic Center Plaza, attended by over four hundred neighborhood officers. I spoke on the topic, 'Appropriate Expenditure of Neighborhood Funds,' and answered questions from the attendees.

After many meeting in the various neighborhoods, the Citizen's Participation Program gave me a trophy, naming me an 'Unsung Hero.' I'm very proud of that trophy, though I guess I'm not unsung anymore, having just sung myself.

 CHAPTER 21

Finally, Some Law Stories

Somebody vs. The City of Birmingham

I don't remember the style of this case, or even what it was about, but I do remember an interesting moment that occurred during the trial.

The plaintiff was represented by Jeffrey William Bennett. Jeff and I had gotten to know each other in prior cases. We became friends, enjoying the competition of trial by jury. One Monday, Jeff and I arrived in court to start a trial. The judge was handling a motion docket at the time, so we sat in the audience benches to wait for our case to be called.

Both of us were music fans. I told him about a book I had just read, *Shakey*, a biography of Neil Young. There was a funny story in the book that I related to him. Neil was living in a home in the country in California. The house was on a hill and the yard sloped down to a pond. On the other side of the pond, the slope went back up hill to where his barn was located. Neil had recording equipment in both the house and the barn.

On one occasion, someone from his record label visited to check on the progress of his next album, which Neil was recording in his home studio. Neil said, "Follow me," and took him down the sloping yard to the pond. Neil asked him to get into a small boat, and then paddled out to the middle of the pond, midway between the house and the barn. Neil yelled, "Ok!" and someone cranked up the music from both the house and the barn, a stereo effect. Neil put his head down, listening for a minute, and then looked up and yelled, "More barn!" Jeff found this to be as amusing as I did.

Our case was called, and we began the trial. The jury was empaneled, opening arguments were done, and now we're calling witnesses. The witness box is always next to the Judge's bench on the side closest to the jury. The plaintiff's table is closest to the jury, and the defendant's table is next to plaintiff's on the side away from the jury box.

This is what I remember about the trial. I had finished my direct examination of one of my witnesses. Turning away from the jury, I started walking back toward my table as Jeff was walking toward me to cross-examine the witness. We were passing each other directly in front of the Judge. As we got even with each other, and without turning my head toward him, I whispered, "more barn."

Jeff lost it. Before he could stop himself, he let out a gigantic laugh. I just kept walking. I don't know how the jury reacted, and the Judge made no comment. Thankfully for me.

We explained the incident to the Judge after the trial was over. He thought it was a funny story too.

Jeff didn't seem angry about my interruption, but I'm sure he was planning how he would pay me back during our next trial.

CHAPTER 22

A Speedy Verdict

Burdine Stutson v. City of Birmingham and Dennis Blass

I remember this trial because of its memorable ending. The case was tried by jury before Judge N.D. Rogers in Jefferson County Circuit Court. The plaintiff, Burdine Stutson, was represented by Oscar Adams III, and John Edens served as my co-counsel in the trial.

The plaintiff had been arrested on a charge of trafficking cocaine by the Birmingham Police Department Vice Squad.

Defendant Captain Dennis Blass was the commander of the vice squad and had been involved in hundreds of drug busts.

On this occasion, the squad had received a tip about a drug deal going down behind a fast-food restaurant. Captain Blass and his crew went to the scene in their unmarked, tinted windowed van to scout the transaction. The officers observed someone toss a package into some bushes behind the restaurant. Shortly after that, Mr. Stutson arrived and retrieved the package. Captain Blass and his officers exited the van and arrested him.

The plaintiff claimed that he was unlawfully arrested, that

the City of Birmingham had a 'custom, policy, or practice' of coercing confessions, and it failed to properly train Captain Blass in the correct methods of interrogating a prisoner. He further claimed the city's policy was unconstitutional and that Captain Blass had coerced his confession. He asserted that the actions of Captain Blass had caused him to suffer emotional distress, mental anguish, and resulted in him losing his job as a high school teacher and coach.

In our defense, we admitted that Mr. Stutson was arrested after a drug buy was completed. The package that he had picked out of the bushes contained three ounces of cocaine. Captain Blass did, as alleged, place a gun against Mr. Stutson's head and yelled curses at him during the arrest.

Captain Blass's testimony went down like this:

Me- "Captain Blass, why were you at this restaurant on this occasion?"

Blass- "I had a tip from an informant about a drug deal that was set up there."

Me- "What happened?"

Blass- "We went to the location of the deal described by the informant."

Me- "What happened next?"

Blass- "I saw an individual toss a package into the bushes and shortly after, observed Burdine Stutson retrieve the package."

Me- "And then?"

Blass- "We exited the van and arrested Mr. Stutson and took the cocaine from his possession."

Me- "Mr. Stutson testified that you placed a gun against his head and loudly cursed him. Did you do that?"

Blass- "Yes."

Me- "Why?"

Blass- "In most drug arrests, the party is armed and has cohorts in the vicinity. Our policy is to rapidly diffuse the situation, particularly because there may be innocent bystanders in the area. Such was the situation at this restaurant. We wanted to keep them safe from violence that could possibly happen while making the arrest."

Me- "How many such drug arrests have you made in your career with the vice squad?"

Blass- "Hundreds."

Me- "And how many times have you used this method of making an arrest?"

Blass- "Almost every time."

Me- "And how many innocent bystanders have been injured during these arrests?"

Blass- "None."

Me- "So the policy seems to work pretty well?"

Blass- "Very well."

Me- "No further questions."

John Edens did a great job with the closing argument for the defense. Judge Rogers charged the jury regarding the applicable law and sent them to the jury room to deliberate.

The trial had lasted four days. Sometimes, after the jury has gone to the jury room to begin their deliberations, there may be a knock on their door shortly after retiring because a juror left something in the courtroom, or they might want to know when they could take their lunch break.

On this occasion, the knock came less than two minutes after they had left the courtroom. The Clerk went to see what they needed, returned to the bench, and advised Judge Rogers that the jury had reached a verdict. Returning to the courtroom, the jury announced that the verdict was in favor of the city and Captain Blass.

We had broken the two-minute verdict. A new world record, maybe.

Captain Blass sent a nice letter to the Mayor and City Attorney, commending our 'stellar performance', and requesting John and I handle the case should he ever be sued again.

Of course we would.

CHAPTER 23

Be Careful What You Eat

Daniel Gary Levan v. City of Birmingham, M. Pettway

On January 14, 1993, at approximately 4:00am, Mr. Levan was driving in the eastern area of Birmingham when he was pulled over by a police officer for speeding. After an investigation, the officer placed him under arrest for possession of illegal drugs and transported him to the Birmingham City Jail. Correctional Officer Pettway was advised of the drug charge before he began processing Mr. Levan into the jail.

Officer Pettway asked Mr. Levan to empty his pockets and place the contents on a table. As Levan was doing this, he put an item on the table, then picked it up and put it in his mouth. Officer Pettway grabbed Mr. Levan and told him not to swallow and to spit out what he had put in his mouth. Levan refused to follow the officer's order. Pettway then took action to try and prevent Levan from swallowing the item, taking him down to the floor, during which Levan received physical injuries, including a broken collarbone. Officer Pettway prevented him from swallowing the item.

Mr. Levan alleged in his suit that, 'the City of Birmingham and its employees had a duty to use reasonable force against him while he was in their care and custody. The actions against him were excessive and unwarranted, and Officer Pettway was negligently trained in his duties.'

Officer Pettway was aware that this arrest involved a drug charge. After the plaintiff rested, I called Lt. Lakey, Officer Pettway's supervisor, to the stand. He testified that the officer followed the jail's policy to prevent an inmate from swallowing any unknown substance while in its custody.

Officer Pettway testified next, stating he was taught to never allow a prisoner to swallow something if the officer did not know what it was. He knew that Mr. Levan's charges included drug possession. When he saw Levan place something in his mouth, he immediately yelled, "Don't swallow that, spit it out!" When Levan failed to do that, he grabbed Levan and placed his hand in a manner to prevent swallowing. Levan began resisting and in the struggle they both fell to the floor, causing the injury to Levan's collarbone.

I asked Pettway, "Why do you have such a policy regarding prisoners, what could happen?"

Pettway- "Mr. Levan was arrested on a drug charge. We process hundreds of these cases every year. It's our experience that in booking them, some have attempted to swallow contraband drugs, sometimes successfully."

Me- "What is the jail's concern regarding such an action? Is it about the loss of evidence?"

Pettway- "The concern is not about the loss of evidence; it

is about the loss of the prisoner's life. Actions like that taken by Mr. Levan have often resulted in an overdose of drugs resulting in injury or death."

Me- "So in that moment, with only a split-second to react, you were trying to prevent a possible overdose and death to Mr. Levan?"

Pettway- "Yes, after he finally spit it out, it was a Rolaids."

All Levan had to do to avoid injury was to follow Officer Pettway's order.

The trial lasted two days and the jury was out for two and a half hours.

They returned a verdict for the defendants.

CHAPTER 24

Americans With Disabilities Act (ADA)

The ADA was passed by Congress in 1990. It is a federal civil rights law that prohibits discrimination against people with disabilities in everyday activities. It provides the same protection as civil rights laws that prohibit discrimination based on race, color, sex, sexual orientation, national origin, age, and religion.

ADA guarantees that people with disabilities have the same opportunities as everyone else to enjoy employment opportunities, purchase goods and services, and participate in state and local government programs.

Title II of the Act applies to all services, programs, activities, and facilities, and their availability to people with disabilities maintained by state and local governments, such as the City of Birmingham. These include public education, transportation, recreation, healthcare, social services, courts, voting, emergency services and town meetings.

The ADA contains specific requirements for state and local governments to insure equal access for people with disabilities.

Title II also covers the City of Birmingham's public buildings, museums, libraries, voting places, sidewalks, and curb ramps.

I was selected to be the ADA Compliance Officer for the City of Birmingham. We were required under the Act to conduct a self-evaluation of our facilities and programs to be completed by July 26, 1992. Then, based on this evaluation, we were to develop a transition plan setting out our ADA deficiencies, both structural and programmatic, and establish a schedule for bringing the city into full ADA compliance.

The U.S. Architectural and Transportation Barriers Compliance Board established the accessibility guidelines covering all physical features of city facilities. Locations included bathrooms, curb ramps, aisle width, handicapped parking, and elevators. The guidelines even set the maximum amount of pressure it would take to open a door. The Act sets forth the measurements and slopes in precise detail for ADA compliance.

This is where I came in.

Access Now, a non-profit organization based in Florida, sent handicapped persons to public and private facilities around the country, inspecting them for ADA compliance. If they discovered a non-compliance problem, Access Now would file suit in federal court. They brought two suits against the City of Birmingham, which were assigned to me.

By me.

After all, I was the ADA Compliance Officer. Plus, I assigned lawsuits in the department, and I was very interested in bringing the city into compliance for its disabled citizens.

Ed Zwilling was the Florida attorney with Access Now representing the plaintiffs in the two suits. We got along great; it was a pleasure working with him to fix the problems his disabled plaintiffs had discovered.

The relief the plaintiffs asked for in these suits was injunctive, meaning we would be required to become compliant with ADA requirements regarding the flaws identified in the suit. The city's goal was always to become totally compliant anyway.

The City Engineer and I inspected the locations in question and planned with the Engineering Department to correct them. The city had been making progress with ADA compliance, but budgetary limitations meant it would take time to fix everything. The two federal lawsuits were settled by a Consent Decree when we made the necessary corrections.

In October 2004, the Department of Justice (DOJ) notified several cities across the country, including Birmingham, that they would be conducting an audit of their facilities for ADA compliance.

Birmingham was required to submit a list of all city properties and facilities open to the public. I coordinated with Andre Bittas in the Engineering Department to collect this information and respond to the DOJ.

After they received our list, DOJ scheduled the audit for December 2004. They divided the city into five sectors and sent a team to inspect each one. Andre and I accompanied the teams on many of their site evaluations, particularly City Hall, the Museum, libraries, and fire stations. The members of the DOJ audit teams were professional, and Andre and I got along with them very well.

To give you an idea of the costs to make required changes, the projected expenditure for bringing the Museum into compliance was over a million dollars. The total audit took two weeks. As an example of why certain facilities were included in the audit, fire stations were inspected because they are used by the public as voting sites in elections.

In coordination with the DOJ, Andre and I developed a transition plan, and identified the necessary funding for correcting the deficiencies as determined by the DOJ inspection.

Addressing the Mayor and City Council to advise them of the Agreement I had reached with the Department of Justice, I said, "We should remember, the ADA is needed and necessary. Compliance must be made because it is the right thing to do for our citizens with disabilities."

Nobody objected. In fact, the city allocated twenty million dollars in bond money and eighty million dollars from the Birmingham Fund to insure we would become compliant.

We made excellent progress in our efforts to bring the city into full compliance. The City Attorney, Tamara Harris Johnson, and I were invited by the DOJ to come to Washington, D.C., telling us they wanted to publicly congratulate the city for the extent of its compliance efforts. At a ceremony in the Department of Justice building, we were honored by the Attorney General.

And then we were given a tour of the White House. This was my second visit to the West Wing. As we were passing the oval office, I remembered walking into this historical room while in the Air Force. So, I stepped into the room on this visit. Several secret service agents suggested that I should leave the oval office.

Which I did.

CHAPTER 25

Oops. My Bad

Somebody, I don't know who, said, "Beware the wrath of the patient man." Being a patient man, I found this to be true wrath-wise.

As I previously mentioned, lawyers with less than five years of experience were referred to as 'baby lawyers.' This isn't a derogatory term; we were all baby lawyers at one time. It just describes the period when a rookie learns in real time how to do this lawyer job.

On one occasion, I was defending the city in a trial before Circuit Judge Rogers. The lawyer representing the plaintiff was a baby lawyer. I was not. Discovery had been completed and I had supplied the plaintiff with everything I had related to the case.

During his examination of the plaintiff, the baby lawyer began implying, through his questioning, that there existed documents favorable to the plaintiff's claims, and further, that I was hiding them from the jury.

And then, the wrath.

I don't remember making a conscious decision to get out of

my chair to physically attack the baby lawyer, but Judge Rogers seemed to sense my intention. As I passed the bench and headed toward the lawyer, I heard the Judge say, quite firmly, "Mr. Melton, stand down."

I stood down.

As I walked back to my seat, Judge Rogers strongly admonished the baby lawyer for implying wrongdoing on my part and instructed the jury to disregard what he had said, while giving me a shout-out. He told the jury that I had tried many cases in his court and that he found me to be an honorable attorney.

After the jury returned a verdict in my favor, the young lawyer approached me and apologized, which I accepted. I then advised him that he should be very cautious in how he made representations to judges and juries. You only get one chance to lose your credibility in this profession, and once lost, you can never get it back.

That's how baby lawyers learn the sport.

I only lost my cool in court on one other occasion. The City of Birmingham and Police Officer Arvin Drake were the defendants in a civil rights suit in U.S. District Court before Judge U.W. Clemon.

The plaintiff was the representative of the estate of Mr. Smith, an individual that had been shot and killed by Officer Drake in the line of duty.

Mr. Smith and his accomplice had robbed a large grocery store on Green Springs Highway in Birmingham. He was armed with a handgun, and during the robbery had fired a shot into the store's ceiling. Then, taking a paper grocery bag, he went to each cashier and ordered them to empty their register into the bag.

The robbers left the store, got in a car, and sped off. The police were notified, observed the vehicle, and pursued it at a high rate of speed. Mr. Smith drove along I-65 into the north area of the city, where he exited the freeway. He sped along city streets, and ultimately drove into a dead-end. Mr. Smith exited the vehicle carrying the paper sack and began running away. The other robber remained in the car, where he was arrested with no resistance.

Officer Arvin Drake got out of his patrol car and drew his weapon. He was aware that Mr. Smith was armed and had discharged his weapon in the grocery store.

Drake ordered Smith to halt and put his hands up. They were approximately fifty feet apart, and instead of following the officer's command, he knelt and reached his hand into the bag. Officer Drake fired his weapon resulting in Mr. Smith's death.

The Birmingham Police Department's Internal Affairs is a unit of the police department that investigates every police shooting to determine if all rules and regulations were followed. If not, an officer is subject to disciplinary action, from time-off without pay, up to firing, and possibly even criminal charges. The unit, after investigation, concluded that Officer Drake's use of deadly force was warranted based on the facts. In police talk, his use of deadly force was 'righteous.'

The plaintiff's suit alleged that Officer Drake violated Mr. Smith's civil rights by shooting and killing him.

I had appeared before Judge Clemon and had the most respect for him. He was always fair and impartial in handling cases in his court. Judge Clemon had been appointed to the federal bench by President Jimmy Carter and had previously been in private practice with my boss, Jim Baker.

In a prior case I tried in his court, Bill Dawson represented the plaintiff. Bill is a good, experienced lawyer and we had tried cases in the past. I remember that Judge Clemon had ordered him not to make a certain statement to the jury. Bill made that certain statement to the jury. Maybe he just forgot. Judge Clemon, however, was not amused. He found Bill in contempt and ordered him to spend the night in jail, which he did.

We both learned what Judge Clemon's limits were. At least I thought I had.

After the plaintiff's attorney and I had completed discovery, I prepared and filed a Motion for Summary Judgment and Judge Clemon set it for oral argument. I appeared in his Court that morning for the motion docket. There were several other attorneys present in the courtroom to argue their motions. Mine was the first called and I went to the podium.

I began setting out the facts of the case that were not disputed. I got to the part where the plaintiff had stopped, knelt, and placed his hand in the paper sack, at which point he was fatally shot by Officer Drake.

That was when Judge Clemon interjected and asked, "Did Officer Drake wait until Mr. Smith pulled out a gun from the sack before he shot him?"

I lost it. Again.

I said, "No, because if he had, instead of Mr. Smith's mother burying her son, it would have been Police Officer Arvin Drake's mother burying her son."

And then, adding insult to injury, I picked up my file, left the podium and sat down. I noticed shocked looks on the faces of the other lawyers in the room. I'm sure they were thinking, "I hope he brought his toothbrush." Remembering that incident with Bill Dawson, I was seriously expecting to spend the night at the government's expense.

Judge Clemon then said, "Mr. Melton, see me after the docket."

I'm thinking, "Was I contemptuous? I bet I was."

After the docket, I approached the bench, immediately apologizing for my conduct. But then, all he said was, "I'm going to tell your boss about this. Your Motion for Summary Judgment is granted."

Later, Mr. Baker spoke to me and said Judge Clemon had told him about the incident. He said they both had a good laugh over it.

Whew.

CHAPTER 26

PETA, MADD, and Me

People For the Ethical Treatment of Animals, PETA, is a good organization, but sometimes they get a little weird.

My first contact with them occurred right outside of City Hall in Linn Park. I could see them from my window on the sixth floor. They had set up a large three-piece board on which they had hung pictures of animals. They also posted pictures of Jewish men in a World War II German concentration camp, and some of the emaciated men were nude.

I got a call from the Mayor's Office that he had received complaints stating the pictures of the nude men were pornographic. He asked me to check it out, so I went to the park and spoke with the PETA people. Matt Prescott was the PETA coordinator and I talked with him about the display. He told me the purpose behind the photos was to show that eating meat was like a holocaust for animals. He called it a 'holocaust on your plate.' Mr. Prescott said further, "If you eat meat, you're similar to nazis."

Cantor Jessica Roskin of Temple Emmanual was present and

expressed to me her opposition to comparing Jewish victims of Hitler to animals.

Kind of a stretch on PETA's part, but to legally declare a picture to be pornographic under the law, it would have to appeal to 'prurient interests,' and these certainly did not. I contacted the mayor and let him know the results of my brief investigation, and PETA was allowed to keep their display.

My second contact with PETA was quite different. The Oscar Meyer Company, PETA's archenemy, had brought their wiener-mobile to Birmingham. This vehicle is shaped like a hotdog and is also called the 'weenie wagon.' They were planning to record their jingle, "Oh, I wish I was an….," never mind, you know how it goes.

Oscar Meyer was going to record auditions by local kids in the director's office at the Birmingham Zoo. I don't think PETA people go to the zoo much, maybe that's why Oscar picked this location. A protest had been organized by Bruce Friedrich of PETA, calling the wiener-mobile a 'mockery of animal suffering.' The weenie wagon was in the zoo parking lot and there were several protesters standing outside of the zoo office windows, loudly chanting.

Once again, I was called to sort it out. I drove to the zoo and went into the office where I found several kids, their parents, the film crew, and a couple of police officers. The protesters were obviously making too much noise for any recording to be made. I noticed that the protesters were standing in a flower bed outside the office. It was about five feet wide, ran the length of the building, and contained flowers and shrubs.

The police officers asked me if they would be within the law if they arrested the protesters for trespass. PETA had many adults and children present, so I found that suggestion problematic.

Then, glancing through the blinds, almost face to face with the protesters, I noticed metal spouts sticking up all over the flower bed and asked the Zoo Director what they were. He said it was the sprinkler system for the flowers and shrubs.

I had a great idea. I asked him what time they came on, and he told me 6:00pm. The current time was 4:30pm.

Then I said, "Can they be turned on now?"

"Yes."

The police officers smiled and pretended they had not heard my proposal. I watched through the blinds as the sprinklers came on and the protesters scrambled out of the flower bed. Shortly after the free shower, they dispersed, and the recording session began.

Well, that worked.

As I was leaving, I saw a lady who was one of the protesters walking with two children to her car. I distinctly heard her ask the kids, "You guys want to go by Taco Bell on the way home?"

I don't think Taco Bell sells vegan burritos.

In the early 1980s, while I was the prosecutor in Judge Hall's court, I tried a DUI case against Carl Bragg, a defendant who had prior such convictions. In this case, he had struck a vehicle being driven by Susan Elaine Mays, a young lady who had just graduated from college. She remained comatose for twenty-one days and had severe scars from the wreck. Judge Hall found Bragg guilty and gave him the maximum penalty available at the time, one year in jail and a five hundred dollar fine.

In Birmingham there was a radio show hosted by Dee Fine and her husband, Dr. Russ Fine. They were an outspoken duo, discussing topics of interest to their audience. They were aware of the Bragg case and expressed their dismay for the limitation on the punishment.

Dee contacted me to discuss the laws governing DUI cases and asked me to assist in making changes to them. Dee said that she was looking into forming a chapter of Mothers Against Drunk Drivers, also known as MADD. She invited me to attend a public hearing at the city's Roebuck Community Center to see if other citizens would support such an organization.

The turnout was huge, and they expressed total support for the creation of MADD. I spoke about the status of penalties for DUI convictions, and what it would take to make them more severe. I also discussed how they could create a 501(c)(3) non-profit corporation under federal tax law.

Dee got the program set up and working, contributing to improvements regarding the penalties that courts had available in handling DUI cases, and keeping the issue in front of the public.

CHAPTER 27

The Klan Wants a Permit

Early in my career with the city law department, I was assigned to draft a new Demonstration and Parade Ordinance for the City of Birmingham to ensure it protected First Amendment rights of free speech and freedom of assembly for all people. The ordinance I wrote required a party to get a permit from the city and pay a nominal fee before their event. The permit application would describe the route they would be taking if for a march in the streets so that roadblocks and escorts could be planned by the city.

The Ku Klux Klan applied for a demonstration permit. Despite my abhorrence for this racist organization, I had to advise the city that legally we would have to issue a permit for their demonstration. I spoke to the Klan's representative who was seeking the permit and advised him the city was reluctantly issuing a permit, and if they became 'threatening or profane' we would shut them down. And, more specifically, do not burn any crosses. He didn't seem to appreciate my warning.

Oh well, can't please everybody.

Prior to the Klan's event, I met with several law enforcement agencies to plan strategy: The Birmingham Police Department, Alabama Highway Patrol, Jefferson County Sheriff's Department, and the local FBI office.

In discussing plans for monitoring the demonstration to ensure the safety of the demonstrators and bystanders, the state trooper asked if we would need to use their helicopter.

Aha!

I remembered my experience in the Air Force, riding in a Huey helicopter, and the incredible noise it made. I asked him if their helicopter was loud. "Very," he said.

Then I asked him how low they were allowed to fly inside a city. "As low as necessary," he replied.

Nothing further on the topic needed to be said.

The big day arrived. The Klan set up a portable stage in Linn Park, which lies between city hall and the courthouse. Their turnout was small, maybe two dozen Klan members, but they still set up a public address system to amplify their speakers' voices. I stood behind the Klan's group with a crowd of counter-protesters that easily outnumbered their participants.

And then, as the first speaker approached the microphone, suddenly a helicopter approached and hovered over the stage.

I was shocked, I tell you. Shocked! It was so loud you couldn't even hear the speaker. They kept looking up at the helicopter, possibly cursing. I don't know for sure; I couldn't hear a word they were saying.

They eventually gave up and started taking down the stage. The copter hovered until it was clear the event was over. The Klan member that I had dealt with about the permit recognized me, approached and angrily objected to the helicopter drowning out their demonstration. I told him, "It was only here for your protection, we're required to do that."

He turned to leave, looked over his shoulder, and called me a 'whigger.'

I'm sure I don't know what that meant.

But enough about that klub.

CHAPTER 28

A Riot at City Hall

Ahmed Obafemi II, et al v. City of Birmingham

The Obafemi case began with a march from Kelly Ingram Park to Birmingham City Hall on January 15, 1994. The group was protesting plans by a private company, Browning-Ferris Industries, to build a garbage transfer station in the Black neighborhood of Titusville on the south-side of Birmingham. The marchers were protesting environmental racism, certainly a very worthy cause.

As I mentioned, under the City's Demonstration and Parade Ordinance, the organizing group Malcolm X Grassroots Movement led by Ahmed Obafemi would need to obtain a permit for the march and provide the route. The permit would have given the city time to provide escorts and block traffic for the marchers to safely parade from the park to City Hall. Mr. Obafemi knew a permit was required to march in the street but testified at trial that he forgot to get one.

The crowd that entered the street to march was made up of

adults and young teenagers. There was traffic on the downtown streets where the demonstrators were marching, which the police would have blocked if the group had obtained a permit.

After marching several blocks, the group turned left onto the street where City Hall was located, three blocks away.

At this point, Birmingham Police Officer Loebler pulled his patrol car in front of the demonstrators, got out, and asked to see their permit to march in the street. When none was produced, Loebler instructed the marchers to move out of the street and onto the sidewalk for their safety, and where no permit was required. Contrary to the officer's order, Mr. Obafemi told the marchers to stay in the street. Using a bullhorn, Mr. Obafemi started a chant of 'kill the cops.'

Officer Loebler attempted to take the bullhorn from Obafemi and arrest him for failing to follow a lawful order. They began scuffling and the marchers continued in the street toward City Hall. Other officers had been notified of the situation and arrived on scene.

At this point, a full-scale riot erupted. Marchers began following Obafemi's lead, assaulting the officers who were trying to control the situation, while cursing and threatening them.

The protesters continued to City Hall, down the stairs, and into the building. At this point, reporters from a local TV station arrived and began filming the riot. Sergeant Charlie Hill, a Black officer in charge of the Department's Riot Squad was called extremely racist names by the rioters.

After several minutes, the officers gained control of the crowd and several protesters were arrested. There were physical injuries to both officers and protesters.

Eventually, the demonstrators who had been arrested had

their charges dismissed by the city. Despite the melee created by the marchers, the city felt the reason they were marching was valid. The organizer forgot to obtain a permit, but the marchers were not aware of that fact, and many of the demonstrators were minors. The city believed this was a fair way to handle the charges.

Apparently, this wasn't satisfactory to Mr. Obafemi and seven of his young marchers who had come from Atlanta to participate in the protest. They filed suit against the City of Birmingham in the U.S. District Court, alleging a violation of their civil rights. They claimed the city had failed to properly train its police officers in how to handle riot control, resulting in injuries to the plaintiffs.

The case came to trial three years after the incident in 1997, and was assigned to U.S. District Court Judge William M. Acker, Jr.

David Gespass represented the plaintiffs in the case. We had known each other for years. I admired him for his work outside of his career as a lawyer. David had been a volunteer on many occasions as an election monitor in foreign countries to help ensure a fair election. These elections occurred in countries where his safety was always in peril.

At the Mayor's suggestion, the city retained the services of Carole Smitherman, an attorney in private practice, to serve as my co-counsel. Carole was a civil rights lawyer. When she was young, she lost her best friend, Denise McNair, in the Sixteenth Street Baptist Church bombing in September 1963.

Both sides completed the discovery portion of the process. We supplied David with all relevant documentation in our possession, including arrest reports and police training standards.

I assumed David had done the same, supplying us with all the documentary evidence in his possession. Both sides had copies of the TV news videos, which only covered the final minutes of the riot.

The City of Birmingham has had a bad reputation in its history regarding civil rights, Things began changing in the 1960s with the passage of the Civil Rights Act, Voting Rights Act, and U.S. Supreme Court decisions such as 'Brown v. Board of Education' voiding 'separate but equal' segregation in public schools. At the time of this incident, Richard Arrington was the city's first Black Mayor. By trial, Bernard Kincaid was mayor, the second Black Mayor of Birmingham. Johnny Johnson was the first Black Chief of Police, and Sergeant Charlie Hill was the first Black supervisor of the Riot Squad.

A jury was selected, and Carole presented our opening argument. The plaintiffs began putting on their witnesses, protesters who had been part of the incident. They called sisters Sekelajah Alghanee and Ntiana Alghanee as their last witnesses. The sisters had been twelve and sixteen years of age at the time of the march. Both sisters testified they were chanting 'killer cops' not 'kill the cops.' The sisters testified that they had suffered psychological trauma because of the actions of the police.

Plaintiffs submitted the TV station video into evidence and the jury viewed it on a TV brought into the courtroom.

I cross-examined Ntiana and asked the following:

Me- "Did you hear the police officer instructing you to leave the street and go onto the sidewalk?"

Ntiana- "Yes."

Me- "What else did you hear?"

Ntiana- "I heard Mr. Obafemi say, stay in the street."

Me- "Which one did you obey?"

Ntiana- "Mr. Obafemi of course."

Then, with no idea what the answer would be,

Me- "Was anybody in your group filming this?"

Ntiana- "Yes."

Me- "Where is that tape?"

Ntiana- "I guess our lawyer has it."

David had made a big error. Such a tape should have been provided to us during discovery. Judge Acker interjected and asked the lawyer a question. "Mr. Gespass, how long will it take you to go to your office and bring back the tape?"

David, knowing he was burned, said, "Not long."

He returned to the courtroom with the tape, and once again the TV was brought in and the tape was played, with none of us sure what it would show.

This was the only time I had ever seen a Judge come down from his bench and sit in the box with the jurors to view evidence.

The tape clearly showed the marchers chanting "kill the cops," along with other loud and consistent jeers and taunts.

The plaintiffs rested.

Carole and I put on our defense witnesses. Former Mayor

David Vann had been in the area inside City Hall where rioters and police were fighting.

Me- "Did you see officers assaulting the rioters?"

Vann- "No, it looked more like the rioters were assaulting the police."

Chief Johnson testified about the training officers received in riot control, and that it met all National Standards.

The Defense rested.

It was now late on Friday, so Judge Acker continued the case until Monday for closing arguments.

Carole had done the opening, so I was going to do the closing, and I spent the weekend working on it. I felt that we had proven that we had not violated the plaintiffs' civil rights, that our training in riot control was appropriate, and the officers' actions were not the cause of the riot and plaintiffs' injuries.

I felt there was fault, but not on the part of the City of Birmingham.

Monday morning, David made his argument to the jury, saying that plaintiffs had proven their claims of civil rights violation by the defendant city. He said the incident was caused by grown police officers assaulting and arresting children.

The video he had forgotten to provide me during discovery showed otherwise.

I then made my most unusual closing. Ever.

Facing the jury, I thanked them for their service. Then turning from the jury, I faced the plaintiffs' table and spoke directly to Mr. Obafemi. I kept expecting Judge Acker to tell me to address my comments to the jury, but he never did.

This is what I said to him.

"All freedoms that the Constitution guarantees must come with responsibility. Without that, we have no rights. If you forget what anarchy is like, look at the tapes."

"When you're responsible for the safety and welfare of children and you're going to put them in the street, Mr. Obafemi, get a permit."

"If you're marching without a permit and you're told by the police to move to the sidewalk, Mr. Obafemi, do it, because that is a lawful order. Do not allow members of your protest to yell 'kill the cops.'"

"When you're teaching children about their rights, Mr. Obafemi, teach them also about responsibility."

The jury was out for an hour and returned a verdict for City of Birmingham.

After the trial, Carole and I received a letter from my boss, City Attorney Demetrius Newton. He said that Judge Acker had called him to congratulate us for our preparedness and outstanding manner in trying the case.

Demetrius said I did the Law Department proud.

CHAPTER 29

Dropping Names

As I mentioned, my 1960s band's original name was Hard Times, which I stole from the Charles Dickens' book. Then our record label made us change the name and I remembered that piece of classical music 'The Rites of Spring.' Thank goodness it was not titled 'Chocolate Umbrella' or something weird.

I have been to many concerts over the years; The Eagles, Bruce Springsteen (eight times), Elton John, James Taylor, The Allman Brothers, B.B. King, Joan Baez, Bob Dylan, Willie Nelson, etc.

And I mentioned some of the artists my band, The Rites of Spring, got to open for or back-up in the 1960s. But there's more.

On August 18, 1965, I went to Atlanta for a concert by this little ole band from England called The Beatles. My ticket stub shows I paid $4.50 to see this group.

No, I couldn't hear them, the crowd noise went beyond individual voices. It was a solid roar, like standing behind the engine of a jet. And yes, they were only on stage for thirty minutes. But it was fabulous, knowing the crowd and I were breathing the same air as John, Paul, George, and Ringo, and that was enough.

Linda and I met many artists that were booked to play her Hoover Library Theater. For instance, Rosanne Cash. She told us about the 'list,' a hundred songs that she should know according to her dad, Johnny Cash. Rosanne later recorded several of these songs in an album titled, of course, 'The List.' Not saying we're close, but she gave us her home address in New York, and invited us to drop in sometime.

One evening, Stephen Bishop played the theater. He wrote a lot of great music, like 'On and On,' and the theme song for the movie 'Animal House.' After the show, he asked Linda and I to take him to get something to eat. At 11:00pm, the only place we could find open was a Chinese restaurant. We got a booth in the otherwise empty place and were having a nice conversation, when Stephen got up and said he would be back. We assumed he was going to the restroom, but twenty minutes later he had not returned. We started looking for our lost singer. As we wandered around, I caught a glimpse of him in the kitchen. When I went in, it turned out Stephen was helping the cooks prepare our dinner. I didn't know you could do that in a restaurant, but I had never been out with Stephen Bishop before.

Linda's Southern Voices Writer's Conference began in 1992 with Rosalyn Carter as the Keynote Speaker. Every February, incredible writers, artists, and musicians appear over an awesome four days in the Hoover Public Library, and I get to meet them. In 1998, my group the Alabama Troubadours provided the music for the Southern Voices show.

Linda's great staff attend other writer's conferences around the country to find authors for the next Southern Voices. I have been fortunate to go on many of these treasure hunts; Atlanta, Nashville, Chicago and other cities sponsoring writer's conferences. In those sojourns, I've gotten to meet people I could not have met any other way, like Brenda Lee ('Rockin' Around the Christmas Tree'), Scotty Moore (Elvis' guitarist), Richie Havens (the opening act at Woodstock), and Molly Ringwald (from Pretty in Pink to jazz singer).

On one occasion in Nashville, Waylon Jennings was discussing his autobiography at the writer's conference. He spoke in a very large auditorium, the first of several writers on the panel. At these conferences, the author after speaking goes to a signing table, usually in a different location, to autograph their book. On this occasion, he was the first speaker, and when he finished, he left the building. The audience, which included his wife, Jessi Colter, remained to hear the other speakers. I followed him out and saw that he was going to the signing tables to wait for his book fans. I thought he wasn't familiar with the way these events were run, that it would be at least an hour before the last panelist spoke and everyone came out. So, I started a conversation, and we talked for an hour. Waylon was kind, soft-spoken, smart, and humble. I got to ask him a question that had been on my mind forever. If Buddy Holly had not died the night Waylon filled in on bass for Joe Mauldin of the Crickets, would he have stayed as Buddy's bass player? He answered, "No, Joe was on his way up from Texas to join him for the next show." The rest is history. Waylon made me feel like we knew each other.

I had a long relationship with the author Pat Conroy. We first met when Linda signed him to be the keynote speaker one year. He wrote *Prince of Tides*, *The Great Santini*, and *Lords of Discipline*, among others. Those three were made into successful movies. On one occasion, Pat was in town with his father, a former Marine fighter pilot, also known as the Great Santini, and the subject of the book by the same name. Pat told us about a long-ago flight when he sat next to a passenger named Frank Stitt. Frank had told him that he was planning to open a restaurant in Birmingham, Alabama. Pat was wondering if that had happened. In fact, he had opened three restaurants: the Highland Bar and Grill, Chez Fonfon, and Bottega. It was around 10:30pm when I called the restaurant and Frank answered. I told him I had a friend who was wondering if he was still open. When I mentioned Pat's name, he said, "Yes, come on down." Pat's father said he wanted to come with us. Pat said "No" and sent the Great Santini back to the hotel.

It was around 11:00pm when Pat, Linda, and I arrived, and noticed there were no other diners in the Highland Bar and Grill. Frank seated us, and when Pat asked for a menu, Frank said, "You don't need a menu, my staff is still here and we're going to give you guys a sample of everything." And they did. We had a long, fascinating conversation while we enjoyed a bite of everything. I remember looking at my watch when we left, it was 2:30 in the morning. Thank you, Frank.

On another one of his visits, we introduced Pat to Sandra King, a novelist from Montevallo, Alabama. It was a blind date, with dinner at our house. They hit it off, and within a year they were married.

Linda and I visited them in South Carolina in 2003. He was a wonderful, talented man. We miss him.

Another keynote speaker at Southern Voices was the former Alabama football coach, Gene Stallings. He was living on his ranch in Texas and arrived at the Hoover Library around 5:00pm that Friday. Gene had written a beautiful book about his son John Mark who had been born with Down syndrome.

Gene wasn't scheduled to speak for three hours and had made arrangements with a promotional company to sign footballs and other memorabilia for sale. I volunteered to take him to the location and sat with him for two hours while he autographed these souvenirs. The most unusual part of our conversation, the word 'football' was never used by either of us. We talked about his ranch in Texas and the special way he grew tomatoes. He drew a diagram for me should I want to use his hydroponic method.

I got him back to the library in time for his presentation.

CLOSING ARGUMENT

Ladies and gentlemen of the jury…

No wait, that's not right.

Readers of my memoir, thank you for performing your civic duty in this case.

That's better.

The legal cases I described are just a few of the many suits I handled over thirty years. Some were settled, others dismissed on Summary Judgment, and many were tried.

The jury trials were my favorite. As I mentioned, it's like participating in sports, trials were a competition between me and the other team, with a judge as the referee. That doesn't mean I did not take these cases seriously; it just focused me to do the best I could for my clients.

Preparation was key. I learned as a baby lawyer that the most prepared attorney had the homefield advantage. And then experience, I learned something in every case I tried that was beneficial to future trials. And every trial was different. Something unexpected happened in almost every one, and when that happened, it made the trial more exciting.

I miss the challenge of trial work, and I am glad I had the opportunity to participate in this profession. Some of the lawyers

I worked with long ago are still at it. I'm looking at you, Richard Jaffe and Emory Anthony.

As much as trial work was rewarding, so was teaching. Getting to share my experiences with students, whether in junior college, seminars, or law school, was a great occupation.

I carried the knowledge and experience gained in each profession from one to the next: musician, Air Force Intelligence Service, mechanic, bond agent, social worker, photographer, teacher, lawyer, and author.

And pilot, I think I forgot to mention that. I got free lessons when I helped the Birmingham Aero Club restore the 1947 Aeronca Chief on display at the Southern Museum of Flight.

I enjoyed all the jobs I got to participate in, and the great people I met and worked with all those years. Everyone has their own definition of success, I have mine.

Success for me was getting up every morning and being excited about what I'm going to do that day. It was the satisfaction of learning a new skill, and then doing the job the best I could. It was always finding something new that just showed up unexpectedly but sounded interesting. And success was not being hesitant to try something new for which I had no experience, with no fear of failure. I knew I was not a genius or a natural talent, I just found out early that if I put in the effort, the time, and the desire, I could do a job as good as those people. And sometimes, maybe better.

But the best gig of all, if I had to select one, I got to make music.

It's the one thing I still do in my own 'Catfish Studio.' Michael Gunnels, every time he comes down to record some demos, tells me there are not enough bass players in Nashville, and asks me to come up and play. The answer this time is not difficult, I tell him 'No.'

So far.

And something special happened a few years ago. Linda and I see Carolyn several times a year, on holidays and birthdays. She is a friend, and Linda and Carolyn refer to each other as their 'wife-in-law.'

So, for anyone reading about my checkered past, as the song says, "When you get the choice to sit it out or dance,"

I hope you dance.

Yes